Walking Spain
A Young Writer's Journal

(1965-66)

by
George Venn

ABOUT THE COVER:
centaur/ionic columns from original 5x6.5" wire-bound journal
blue ink doodles by Elizabeth
map from original *National Geographic*—red lines mark travel routes
original passport photo from 1965 (back cover)

Copyright © 2023 by George Venn

All rights reserved. This book or any portion thereof may not be reproduced or used in any manner whatsoever without the express written permission of the publisher except for the use of brief quotations in a book review.

Printed in the United States of America

Hardback ISBN-13: 978-1-946970-15-2
Paperback ISBN-13: 978-1-946970-16-9
Library of Congress Control Number: 2023915476

First Edition: November 2023

Published by
Wake-Robin Press
An imprint of redbat books
La Grande, OR 97850
www.wakerobinpress.com

Cover & Book Design: Kristin Summers | redbat design | www.redbatdesign.com

...for the lovers who
por los amantes que
let their dreams depart
dejan sus sueños viajar...

—Greenfields

Table of Contents

Introduction 1

Chapter 1: Spokane to New York 9
October, 1965

Chapter 2: New York to Lisbon 21
October, 1965

Chapter 3: Salamanca Days 29
October, 1965

Chapter 4: Salamanca Fall 49
November, 1965

Chapter 5: Salamanca Winter 65
December, 1965

Chapter 6: Salamanca to Lisbon 79
January, 1966

Chapter 7: Lisbon to Valencia 103
January, 1966

Chapter 8: Valencia to Alicante 121
January/February, 1966

Chapter 9: Saler to Orgaz 139
March/April, 1966

Chapter 10: Orgaz to Seville 151
April, 1966

Chapter 11: Madrid to Southhampton 163
April, 1966

Chapter 12: London to Spokane 177
April/May/June/July, 1966

Selected Works 211
About the Author 213

De todos los libros en el mundo, las mejores historias
se encuentran entre las paginas de un pasaporte.

Of all the books in the world,
the best stories are found between the pages of a passport.
—ANON

* * *

Viajar, dormir, enamorarse son tres invitaciones a lo mismo.
Tres modos de irse a lugares que no siempre entendemos.

Traveling, sleeping, falling in love are three invitations to the same thing.
Three ways to go places we don't always understand.
—ÁNGELES MASTRETTA

* * *

La única regla del viaje es: no vuelvas como te fuiste.
Vuelve diferente.

The only rule of travel is: don't come back as you left.
Come back different.
—ANNE CARSON

Introduction
April
2023

VERTICAL FROM UPPER LEFT:
Marine Travel Reply, NYC, '65
Ecuador Banana boat, FL, '64
Marine Travel card, NYC, '65
Dorn in Chekhov, ID, '65
Joe Sander family, WA, '65

VERTICAL FROM UPPER RIGHT:
Summer Logging, Pack Forest, WA, '65
Mayo Grandparents Alder, WA, '65
title of literary magazine, ID, '65
literary mag cover photo By Jan Boles, ID, '65

4-23-23 Introduction

When Covid came lurking in 2020, I hunkered down with shots and boosters while health and disease warred around me. Ironically, those days of quarantine became normal literary solitude—more time to gather, transcribe, and organize the unexpurgated manuscript presented here: my first journal, *Walking Spain (1965–66)*. Through 2020 and most of 2021, I worked in isolation until bone-on-bone pain in my left hip persuaded me to have surgery. On November 2, 2021 a Portland surgeon "replaced my hip," then admitted me to the hospital. I didn't awaken for a shocking 48 hours. My faithful son stayed by my side those nights, said I babbled incoherently, caused alarm, went limp, resisted a foam monster, tore off catheters, fought Japanese restraints. Reputed for being free and easy, this hip replacement nightmare was neither.

While *Walking Spain* languished half done on my desk in La Grande 300 miles away, dumbfounded medical professionals in Portland finally labeled my symptoms encephalopathy, post operative dementia, mental fog, and sent me to rehab. There, at 78, I relearned the toiletry of childhood. I stuttered. My handwriting turned to scrawl. I felt like crying all the time, wanted to play a piano. My left hand couldn't remember the keys. I learned wheelchair. Around Christmas, a Portland neurologist rendered her verdict: "Parkinson's is clearly in play… So park your car, stop driving, no more cycling, start taking medication, come back in six months." *Walking Spain (1965–66)* would be delayed.

By 2022, after months in slow rehab, weeks of therapy, and walker walks, I felt a compelling need to start writing again, to share that life I knew nearly 60 years ago, a time of adventure and energy and discovery. If I could just concentrate enough to read and transcribe this journal, these 90-some texts might offer more salutary steps to recovery. Wondering if I could still write anything, I began the following introduction, trying to help myself remember where *Walking Spain* began—in Ecuador, 1964.

* * *

Standing on the Guayaquil waterfront dock, I watched sweating muscular black stevedores pack stalks of green Ecuadorian bananas up a gangplank ramp and into the refrigerated hold of the *MV Calanca*. Loading that sleek white banana boat looked dangerous and difficult. I knew I couldn't do it. Harry Belafonte's "Banana Boat Song" came to me there. Almost out of money that spring of 1964, I found Captain Polle on deck, presented myself as a broke student going home. In exchange for typing inventory and scraping paint on his Dutch ship, he gave me free passage for the seven-day voyage to Florida. What luck!

By dusk, the hold was packed with green bananas, sealed against tropical heat, vipers, and tarantulas. My suitcase and Olivetti stashed on board, we sailed with the tide down the roiling brown Guayas River to the Pacific, then north three days up the coast to the Panama Canal entrance. We anchored offshore, then cruised another day through the Canal itself—the only day I wasn't seasick—then three more days across the blue Carribbean—flying fish landing on deck, porpoises leading the way to Florida. Landing in Tampa after living and working for nine months in Quito, Ecuador's Andean capital, I had just enough cash to buy a chocolate shake, a loaf of Wonder bread, and a hungry three-day Greyhound ticket across the United States to Spokane, Washington.

Living in Ecuador my 21st year (1963–64) had changed me. Politics, coup, street riots, a mounted police charge, a tear gas attack on student demonstrators—all that chaos had cancelled my Central University classes. Machine gun posts guarded university buildings. Trucks of armed soldiers held main intersections in the city. With my days suddenly free from formal study, I set out to discover the rich and ancient and diverse culture around me: found new bilingual friends among the girls, radio announcers, and staff at a nearby station, improved my spoken Spanish, taught English to night classes of Ecuadorians for the United States Information Agency, sang in choirs on local television in English and Spanish, coached the Alliance High School basketball team, learned to drink beer, played clay-court tennis. Evenings, I began a new practice—writing long letters home on my blue-green portable Olivetti. "I like this being international," I wrote my parents, "maybe I won't come back." Living alone, making all my own decisions, writing letters—a profound new sense of self and freedom was growing. I could never go back to being that smart, athletic, musical, monocultural, monolingual Protestant kid from the north Idaho sticks. A chrysalis was disappearing.

Returning to the College of Idaho for the 1964–65 year, I felt constrained by the traditional textbook-and-lecture education. At 21, Ecuador had shown me another way: I could actively engage culture, texts, places, and people. I wanted to keep learning more about Hispanic culture, to continue to have adventures like Lazarillo, the main character I'd met in the pages of *Lazarillo de Tormes*, the first and only picaresque novel I'd read. So, while declaring an English major and again taking traditional degree courses, including Spanish Literature, I read Juan Ramon Jiminez' *Platero y Yo* and Miguel Unamuno's *The Tragic Sense of Life*, and set out to surreptitiously create a second year abroad—this time in Spain. Making up a fictitious scholarship, telling no one about my plans, I researched jobs on ocean freighters, corresponded in Spanish with the University of Salamanca, contacted shipping companies, finally booked passage on the Italian Line from New York to Lisbon, and discovered the night train to Paris would stop in Salamanca long enough to let me deboard.

Plans for a picaresque adventure completed in mid-April 1965, I wrote my pious older brother a letter summarizing my busy end-of-sophomore-year: reading in Cervantes, Shakespeare, Robert Penn Warren, acting as Dorn in Chekhov's *The Seagull*, editing *Prospectus*, the college literary magazine. In the final paragraph, I invited him to travel with me and confessed my fabricated cover story (see back cover).

* * *

July 2021, Covid still lurking. Months of rehab completed, I was deep into daily reading and transcribing when my new doctor gave a new diagnosis: I had Lewy Body Disease—an incurable and mysterious "nervous system disorder characterized by a decline in intellectual function (dementia), a group of movement problems known as parkinsonism, visual hallucinations, sudden changes (fluctuations) in behavior and intellectual ability, and acting out dreams while asleep (REM sleep behavior disorder.)"

What could I do? Could I even finish *Walking Spain?* Dr. "O," the new neurologist reduced my prescription. I still could not walk without a walker. I lost all mobility except a small electric scooter. I moved into assisted living. Did what therapists asked. My leg was weak. With the help of friends and family and caregivers, I kept working on *Walking Spain*. From three months in Salamanca I scanned first drafts typed on my Olivetti, then digitized pages from my bound journal *Notes for Iphigenia*. From seven months wandering on the road, I transcribed longhand from small spiral notebooks (see front cover). Once in London, I had taken up writing with the Olivetti again. In all of this recovery and conversion I did not revise or edit for sophistication or literary merit. I wanted readers to feel the same surprise I felt when re-reading my original crude beginnings, an unexpurgated journal of travel, a narrative collage by a virginal 21-year-old Idaho kid living and walking and hitchhiking the towns and roads and highways of Spain, Portugal, and England.

By August 2022, transcription was done. I'd survived, was ready to share this journal—ninety-some unpublished texts transcribed during Covid (2020–2023) and Lewy Body Dementia. Except for a few typed letters to and from home and excerpts from the press in Eatonville, WA and Caldwell, ID, all are unedited and copied from original sources—except for final sharp-eyed proof reading by Greg Johnson. To enrich the visual record for the reader I also include memorabilia—official logos from the ocean liner, railroad stationery, a Spanish calendar, postcards, and personal photographs.

Dressed in jeans, hiking boots, waterproof jacket, and straw Panama hat, I sheltered anywhere in a cream-colored Eddie Bauer tent—external frame, no fly—and slept anywhere on the ground in a blue Himalayan Pack Company sleeping bag with a raw silk liner. I shouldered a gray Spanish rucksack, a canteen, hunting knife, a propane stove, and gear for the road: dishes, cookware, notebooks, clothes, and food. Following Lazarillo's trail, I was another innocent abroad out to discover and explore the world. Along the way, the astute reader may find the seeds of my future writing and editing: (1) appreciation of regional cultures referred to by Unamuno as "intrahistory"—the daily life of people; (2) wealth of cultural regionalism and pluralism; (3) the rewards of being bicultural and bilingual; (4) the quest for love, justice, and truth; (5) the value of embracing the eclectic complexity and diversity of literary genres. I give you just the raw journey and the uncorrected record, fixing only confused or intrusive mechanical errors.

By September 2022, Kristin Summers of Redbat Creative and I had negotiated a book design contract that included her composing the colorful and ingenious chapter break collages and for directly supporting the formation and production of this collection. A book such as this would be impossible without her steady and congenial support as well as the encouragement of many others to whom I want to give my thanks. Pictured in other collages you will find my Alder grandparents George and Hazel Mayo who gave me the summer of free room and board so I could save all my paychecks from Joe Sander the savvy Alder gyppo logger who paid me $2.00 an hour as a laborer for that summer. Without their support I could never have made the journey recorded here. My parents Frank and Beth Venn also played a major supporting role by sending me a perfect tent for the road and keeping up a regular correspondence. In Salamanca, the Fulgencio Sanchez family made every effort to provide a comfortable room, a writing table, a bracero to warm my shins, and congenial family stories and meals. I want to gratefully acknowledge all the drivers in Spain who saw my thumb in the air and stopped and shared their stories. The red flash of those brake lights always cheered my wandering soul.

En el coche de San Fernando
George Venn (1943–   )
La Grande, Oregon
4/23/2023

1.
Spokane to New York
October
1965

VERTICAL FROM UPPER LEFT:
Metropolitan Program, '65
USSR Statue UN, '65
Tapestry UN, '65
train map, '65
train schedule, '65

VERTICAL FROM UPPER CENTER:
Bonsai Exhibit, CO
Train Stationery
Railroad History
Train Schedule
Philadelphia Museum

VERTICAL FROM UPPER RIGHT:
Trident Theater Program, CO
Franklin Statue, PA
Philadelphia, PA
Train History, OR/WA

9-25-65 Spokane to Hinkle on #298

My escape complete. Outside, afternoon harvest under way, I'm clanking south through Palouse hills riding the only 3-car train in the territory: engine, coach, caboose. Two years I've ridden to college in Caldwell on this short train hardly anyone rides. Remember that ancient brakeman. Says railroaders named this train the "City of Hinkle" a joke to offset its diminutive size. Yeah, I think—words can make all the difference. And numbers too—big number 298 on the engine leading the way to the desert junction and that lonely block building surrounded by sand where the Union Pacific main liner "City of Portland Rose" will come roaring in from Oregon, stop with a thousand hissing hoses and squealing steel wheels, rescue us from sweat in the waiting room, and carry us east as the sun goes down. Heart in my throat, I'm ready to leave this middle of nowhere.

```
9-26-65 City of Portland Domeliner, Hinkle to Denver
```

*A*nonymous is waiting for me at the Denver station, lover and bright poetic friend from college. We hug and brush lips. I don't know what she's planned beyond her favorite sloe gin cocktail. Her voice is subtle and low and our history in the dorm includes her panties and the possibilities of love, but I don't know what she wants now. Her poems I published were full of repressed passion but always "Anonymous." After dinner, she's bought tickets for the Trident Theater production of *Telemachus* by Lewis John Carlino. "Tel, Tel, go to Hell," the actors chant. I don't know the story very well. Don't know where I am. The play's set in the western US. There are nine actors portraying seventy different characters. I'm tired. I reach for her hand. One intermission, the show's over. She's reserved a motel. We go, foreplay takes over. She wants me but is shy and I'm shy too. I'm a naive 21-year-old virgin. Naked beside me in bed she says "How do we do this now?" I pretend to know. In the morning she takes me to the depot. We promise to write, she kisses me farewell. The wheels squeal, the coupling cars sound departure. Engine rolling eastward, we wave. Layover over. I leave the ambiguous Rockies behind.

9-27-65 City of Portland Domeliner, Denver to Philadelphia

The road from Spokane to Spain is a long, rhythmic, winding song of duple and triple meter on tracks of ribbon and steel. Ties flash faster than a man can count, while miles disappear, engulfed in darkness and sleepless nights, time zones, and traveling faces illuminated by the blue lights of passenger aisles. Train meets train in the night, man meets man, and their meetings are hectic, short-lived, and noisy in the club car where the Negro bartender makes a gambler's rose, deals another hand, recounts his exploits. Vibrations, flash and roar, massage of miles, thick smoke and pockets of cold air between cars: all lead to the cavernous depot that lives like a bonsai plant, unchanged and still alive and used from an era when the railroad was the lifeline to a new and sprouting west. Raucous laughter of the high student, innocent smiles of naive brown-eyed girls in the dome car, and visions of the parties in roomettes and compartments: we are transient, all, leaving at 1:00 in Omaha, 3:00 am in Altoona. No one ever stays. The moving picture scenery of Wyoming and Colorado flies by in a flash of vanilla and chocolate ice cream snow and dirt. Houses scattered along the tracks, the other side of the tracks. Other houses face away from the tracks, their back yards crawl with rusty car bodies and garbage beside the whispering steel.

New sailors who already hate marines hate playing war games and will never know the thought behind their bullets. Old grandparents and retired men and wives sleeping in discomfort under blankets they brought from home and eating peanut butter sandwiches out of paper sacks filled from their pantries. Discontented, anxious, fidgety, expectant we stare out into the beauty of the landscape and never see or love or identify with the people we pass who wave at the roaring monster passing at the crossing where cars wait, lights flash and bells jangle in the night. Men working by the track, gandy dancers, Negro children throwing rocks at the wheels, old men waving canes in salute, and all the local cars stopped while the once-a-day passengers roar past an otherwise tranquil crossing. Professional porters, conductors, trainmen always asking in detached and austere manners in cold blue, looking for tickets, punching with cold eyes and stiff fingers at the poor paper. Towns fly by, time is the watch on a gold chain in the blue conductor's vest pocket. He asks, the people respond. Train horn sounds three blasts. Tracks beat their tune: I am going, I am going, I am going, never never, rain in Spain, war in America, steel humpty-dumpty, hickory dickory, poor sailor, scotch and water, water and beer, drink a crib, mamma mamma manna—the beat of the steel wheels passing in the night—a never-ending drumming on the ribbon rails.

9-28-65 Philadelphia Station

Tired of rattling trains, so decided to take a short rest here this morning. Sitting in downtown Philadelphia park absorbing the silence. Looked around for founder William Penn, found him in bronze on top of city hall. He's a little overweight at 53,523 pounds, and his hat is the highest point in the city—547 feet above the pavement. He's above the fray. Ascended William Penn by elevator. Wrote postcards home.

Now surrounded by fat pigeons and people and falling leaves. Remember all the leaves to rake at home, the burn piles, baking apples in foil with red hots. That spring I raked all the leaves in Spirit Lake park so I could buy a bus ticket to Seattle to see my then girlfriend Kathy Blackwood.

Found my friend Suzie Good at her Philly nursing school. Short visit between classes—no more. Petite, short, witty but no kisses for me. Knew her from summer date in Alder. Will arrive in NYC 4:30 this pm. Tired, anxious, excited, anticipating only good. Will call tonight. Spain comes closer at each turn of the ship's propeller.

9-29-65 New York, Pennsylvania Station

The throbbing center of the world, its cold steel and cement heart on an island, received me with little more than a rasping cough and screech of wheels. It was too huge for me, too much for two eyes and one head to comprehend, so with suitcase under one arm, my Olivetti under the other, my hands clutching paper bags and raincoats, I stepped out into the Mississippi of humanity where I would have been swept away but for a handy and friendly stone bench where I rested out of the current. There, butt cold on stone, I sat and watched the masses go by, a staring cold world, a preoccupied world, crowds of human beings looking, searching, staring, hurrying down their routes to subterranean tunnels, to waiting subways, to a riot of rush hour cabs negotiating the loud endless river of traffic. Not my world.

When I looked upward to see the sky, endless buildings—high rise monuments of steel and concrete and stone and glass and rivets and thousands of cubicles. I imagined peering down in fear and awe at the street and smog below. All I could think of was old growth forests and Mt. Rainier. Got into a weird conversation with the cabbie. He thought I said "Iowa" when I said "Idaho." Doesn't like New York but can't leave. Never heard of logging. When I said "Washington," he thought I meant "DC." Pretended he couldn't change my $10, then told me to "check my change" for the ride—a tacit request for a tip. When I got out, he cussed me as a hick from the sticks. I laughed.

I walked over to Broadway and 42nd until I came to this face on a billboard blowing smoke rings. Thought about Dorn and Tolstoy and God. Maybe we are God's smoke rings? He takes a deep drag, then exhales and the smoke escapes and we sail out into the world until a draft from some unseen force destroys our shape and the floating circle of our lives disintegrates, is engulfed in a sea of air, gaseous fumes, carbon monoxide, and is no more. Maybe we are all vented smoke rings floating around, mixing with the atmosphere, attempting identity. To escape the hubbub, I caught another cab. My college friend John Perkins lived on Fifth Avenue across from Central Park. John was back in Caldwell, but his parents were expecting me. A bellman in uniform called Mrs. Perkins on the intercom.

9-30-65 New York, Mean Literary Agency

Good days. Lived with the Perkins, wandered the Guggenheim, Empire State Building, Manhattan Island. Admired the Russian gift to the United Nations—a muscular nude man, hammer raised in his right hand and broadsword in his left, the sculpture titled "Man Beating Sword into Plowshare." Watched a bearded man demonstrate with a white flag before the UN—no nationalistic logo. Reading about Albert Schweitzer.

Yesterday, found a literary agent Daniel S. Mean. Gave him my new *Prospectus*. Today, we met face-to-face in his office. With sweating palms and pounding heart, I learned I should consider myself to have talent, that what I had written was not a short story but a character sketch, and that I should not waste further time on arty things but give the public something new, something different, something spicy that would sell big instead of just be appreciated by a few. His comments threw me down the elevator. I was lost. What should I do? I didn't know.

Riding the Broadway bus toward Perkins' flat, I started to wonder aloud: Why don't people here visit with each other? The girl sitting next to me could obviously reply, and if she didn't, then I knew she probably wouldn't want to talk. I detest reticence. "I don't know," she whispers, "but ever since childhood my mother taught me not to speak to strangers and to never take candy from anyone, even a baby."

"But that's no reason not to speak to anyone," I said. Everyone just sits and silently stares out the bus window, as though encased in deep thought—no glances, no surprises, no passing venues.

Even the driver keeps silence except "Keep your ticket in your hand," "No stopping until 86th Avenue, 15 cents please," and repeats the same thing over and over as if he were a broken record in the corner of some sad cafe. Waiting at the light, he frees a life saver from its foil and, after laying it carefully in the palm of his hand, opens the intended morsel and it disappears amid a flash of lips, tongue, and rows of ivory teeth peppered with silver. I hear him talking to himself in monosyllables of discontent, cursing the passengers and the day he turned down that offer to go upstate to farm. He is caught too, caught in a personal trap of discontent and frustration. As he zigzags in and out of Manhattan traffic on a rainy October morning, the great indifference sets in with all its silent glue.

2.
New York to Lisbon
October
1965

VERTICAL FROM UPPER LEFT:
Cristoforo Columbo ship logo and letter typed
  on blue stationery
UN building/NYC skyline

VERTICAL FROM UPPER RIGHT:
Olivetti Portable
Barbara Hepworth sculpture, UN, NYC

10-5-7-65 On Board *Christoforo Colombo*

Met Jacqueline, daughter of a Portuguese fisherman returning to Portugal with her parents where her father is soon to die. She's unskilled, twenty, provocative, mysterious, brown-eyed—a whirlpool of chocolate pudding. Spent several nights on deck with Jacqueline talking about love. She was concrete and candid and honest—never been in love but still willing and ready and unafraid. I'm full of abstractions—too much reading in Fromm's *The Art of Loving*—and I'm still infatuated from my stopover affair and surprise sex in Denver. So we scribbled and passed questions and answers back and forth by running lights along the deck.

One night after talking under the stars she said," You sound very naive when you talk of love. Have you ever loved?

"Went steady for almost two years in high school," I replied.

"That's real puppy love," she laughed. She couldn't see me blushing in the half dark.

"Maybe I could visit you once I'm settled in Salamanca?"

"Good idea. I'll give you my uncle's address at his pension. We'll be staying with him for the first month or so: *Jacqueline Almeida c/o Jose Costeira/ Pensao Costeira/ Pardelhas*. Let's keep in touch."

I was hungry for kisses but couldn't tell her that I loved her.

Tomorrow morning Lisbon, Portugal, and by tomorrow night in Salamanca. The ocean is as close as I can come to comprehending infinity. Shades of indigo and obsidian, the effluvia of the wake, the boundless motion make me feel small and insignificant. Quarters are well below the water line in a cabin with 2 Italians, one Arab from Jerusalem, a Jordanian who studied at the University of Montana, an overconfident, self-satisfied Catholic Italian with an MA in electrical engineering. Italian is the language of the boat, and their culture is the pervading influence. Dinner appetizers are pickled herring, salami, deviled eggs, olives, spiced vegetables, dinner is minestrone or pasta, sliced meat, fried potatoes, ice cream, coffee, fruit. Food is redundant, but Dramamine keeps me from being seasick. Trusty yellow pills. Red wine, much talk (small) and a life of *dolce vita*—vapid yet entertaining. Never a dull linguistic moment. Pretentious crew, a stratified boat, and a ludicrous life boat drill—we all would have drowned had it been real—were most interesting. Passed the Azores yesterday at noon. Saw a lonesome dove, another land bird, and many strange sea birds on deck. When land comes that close after 5 days at sea, you almost want to jump off and swim toward it. One old man refuses to go downstairs to eat or to his cabin to sleep. He has worked 40 years in the States, sent money home, and is now returning to his 75-year-old wife. Fear keeps him on deck all night. He eats pizza and beer for dinner and all the Italians are upset.

10-8-65 Landing at Lisbon, Sud Express to Salamanca

First images of Portugal: colossal concrete statue of Christ, massive unfinished bridge, polluted Tagus River. Misty and cool. Jackie gave me her address and we hugged goodbye, promised to meet again. Customs was easy bribes. For 50 cents, three quick chalk marks and you're inspected. Got a taxi tour of Lisbon. Burly driver thought I was rich, garbled his English until it was time to pay. Got real fluent in a hurry. Bought him lunch. Hit the tourist spots—castles, boulevards, statues, bull rings, cafés. Caught the afternoon Sud Express to Salamanca. From my first class compartment, watched the passing sundown countryside. Fell asleep. Woke in the dark—French seamstress on one side, half drunk Portuguese on the other, spinster across the aisle, another lady asleep. Man dying of cancer on my right offered me swigs from his jug of grape juice. Night at the Spanish border, the train stopped and the customs agent—no notice to me—threw my two locked suitcases off the train. When Don Quixote across the aisle told me, I jumped off the train, sprinted up the tracks, threw my bags back in the baggage car. Customs demanded I open one for inspection. In the dark I dropped my footlocker/suitcase keys, found them, got inspected, then ran and caught the train as it rolled into Spain. What am I doing here? I was finding out.

Left the compartment to stretch between cars. Tried to see into the Spanish night, watched the moon emerge now and then from behind the marble clouds, casting yellow rays on the passing landscape. Pondwater reflected the dying grass. Now and then, the lights of a town would flash by—flickering, faint, gone. We arrived at Salamanca at 11:30. Boom, boom, bamm—my suitcases and I hit the cobblestones. Yellow lights suffused the station and the taxi driver filled me in on the pensions available. I chose the *Perla Salamantina*. Spent a sleepless night on a uncomfortable bed in a windowless black room. Haunted by cat fights, weird faint screams, memories of Jackie and people I knew back home. Finally, unrolled my sleeping bag and fell asleep. A bare light bulb suddenly went on—breakfast time. I walked to the University to ask about housing; they gave me a list of addresses and names. I took the first one—room and board with the Sanchez family. They rented a spare second story bedroom—one large window facing east above *Avenida de la Paz*. Moved my gear, settled in. Live now within sight of the River Tormes, Register tomorrow.

3.
Salamanca Days
October
1965

VERTICAL FROM UPPER LEFT:
Spanish Calendar
registration/receipt
U. of Salamanca, '65

VERTICAL FROM UPPER CENTER:
Spanish Calendar
typed journal on train
stationery, '65

VERTICAL FROM UPPER RIGHT:
Spanish Calendar
Rio Tormes, '65
Domeliner logo, *City of Portland*

10-10-65 Avenida de la Paz #16-2, First AM

The minute my feet hit the floor that morning I knew I was not at home. Dressing quickly in the semi-darkness of 7:00 am, I rose, groped over what seemed acres of dressing table until my hands rested on the familiar surface for which I searched. Then slowly I slid toward my door, opened it and padded the two steps across the hall where the john waited patiently for the morning rush. At first, it seemed like a thousand other mornings. I entered and automatically grabbed at the cold wall where the light switch should be. Not there. Not to be found. Then it jumped out of the wall at chest level.

What is a light switch doing clear up here? Fumbling with the little switch I clicked it twice both ways. Nothing happened. If that one doesn't work, there must be another one someplace. Probably over there around the corner in front of the mirror. I slid my feet along the floor, my hand crawled the wall like some monstrous spider searching for the switch. Then I collided with the sink. Ouch. Somewhere here there's got to be a light. These people can't live in darkness and still shave and comb hair. Maybe they stay in bed until the sun's up. This can't be. Mr. Sanchez goes to work at 9:00, that I know for a fact. Maybe it's over on this side. Groping some more, my hand finally rested on a round switch. Click. Blinded with light. Blinking, fighting the rays, and finally I just closed my eyes and stood there seeing red through the lids. Well, at least there's a light. Great.

Now for some hot water and soap to wash the residue from last night off my face. Great feeling, that first hot washcloth filled with soap and steam. So I bent down and looked at the faucets lettered F and C, big brass fixtures shaped like hooked noses in a Disney picture, and I wondered what happed to the hot water, then remembered where I was. I may have been sleepy, but not that sleepy. Ya: *frio* and *caliente*, I chuckled and patted myself on the back for thinking in Spanish so early in the day. Reaching down, I spun tho four points of the compass on faucets C and stuck a testing finger under the water. Burrrr. Cold. Should warm up in a minute. Too bad the pipes aren't copper like the ones in the new house I worked on last summer. So I stood, waiting a few seconds, then stuck my finger back under the stream. Still cold? What the hell? Maybe they've mixed up the faucets like some homemade plumbers do. I try the faucet F. Spin, white on porcelain, and again I waited with expectant fingers, hoping for hot water to wash my face. None came so I tried the C again and then resigned myself to the fact that there wasn't any, so, hands cupped beneath the C in anticipation that it would suddenly turn warm just as I was about to throw it on my face, I felt the shock of the day and whoosh—ahhhhhh, God, thats cold. Towel, where's the towel? Now where in the hell is that towel? A blind man would have laughed, I'm sure as I found it and dried my whiskered face.

Guess maybe I should shave. Plugin? There on the wall in front of me was a fixture with four round holes which looked like a receptacle for some sort of machine. So I reached into the friendly depths on my shaving kit and caught the Sunbeam Shavemaster by the head, pulled, and the cord snaked out. Well, now what? I see the plugs are different. Now what the hell am I going to do? I've got this electric razor and the damned plug doesn't fit. What kind of a place is this anyway? No hot water, light switches at eye level, lights at eye level, switches that don't work, and now receptacles that don't fit. God, what else can there be wrong! I almost wanted to cry. Then I felt my tongue, sort of thick and heavy with tobacco, and the teeth around it were kind of fuzzy too. Well, guess I have to wait to shave, but I can brush my teeth. Colgate and green brush came out of the kit, unscrew, squeeze, white paste snakes on bristles, toothpaste ala mode, yes breakfast too. (Vitamins—be sure to take them.) Screw back on, twirl the faucet, foam at mouth. Swish, swish, gurgle, rinse, swish, gurgle, expectorate (I would have written spit but that's vulgar), brush, look in mirror at front teeth, back and forth, no up and down like the dentist said, all around the mouth, hum some from a song, try and whistle and then I realized what was happenings There in the bowl was a foaming mass on water and Colgate soda that wasn't draining, Now what the hell is wrong? The drain plugged? I looked underneath the sink and there was a p-trap half as big as it should have been with a bend that would insult a constrictor. I wonder if it works? So I watched the side of the bowl and sure enough, like some viscous mixture of honey and gear oil, it slowly drained away. So, on with the brush, brush, brush, garble, spit. Great tasting stuff that Colgate.

That finished, I squatted down to look into the mirror. Probably could comb my hair a few times, just for practice. I excavated the comb and a blob of Alberto VO5 from the tube, Alberto, now that's a good thing to have in a country that speaks Spanish, and gave the hair the business: comb, comb, part, smell the VO5 and the stale smell that suddenly whammed my nostrils closed. I went over to the toilet and looked for a lever. There wasn't any. Then I examined the wall in front of me and there, hanging from a chain was a little handle. Ah, yes, now I remember. Grandma used to have one of these gravity jobs. So, I jerked the lever and the roar was deafening. Scared the comb right out of my hands. Following my curiosity after picking up the comb, I inspected the plastic seat for contour fit, but cold, cold, cold. The paper placed at a good level was sort of parchment, like that correctible stuff we used at school for term papers and lots of mistakes. A seven-foot bathtub off to the right and down a mountain of porcelain into the depths where there was no plug. Hexagon brass faucets four in two rows, and huge projecting showerhead. What an irony without hot water. No curtain, no soap dish. I wonder if, they ever use this, or if it might be a status symbol with an extremely conspicuous black spider crawling around the bottom. Better finish combing this mop. So I went back to the sink, bent down so I could see in the mirror, and finished the job, parted, primped, perfect except for the cowlick in back that I knew was standing up and I could do nothing about or see. Ah, yes, don't forget the vitamins. I have this very sweet aunt who bought me three bottles of pills before I left. So I clenched the bottle, gave the lid a twist, dropped one of the huge green peanuts into my palm, closed the bottle, gave the pill a heave toward the back of my throat, swallowed and that was it. I replaced all the goodies in the drop kit except for the spray deodorant. "If rash develops discontinue use." After that shock to warm armpits, I flipped off the light and walked to the door, turned the I-shaped handle, and ran straight into Senora Theodora.

"Buenas dias, Don Jorge, Como esta? Has encontrado todo que necessitas? El desayuno sera listo en poco tiempo."

"Gracias, Senora. Tu estas muy amable." I wonder what she's going to do in there without any directions.

I went back to my room across the hall and waited for breakfast of *cafe con leche con pan y mantequilla*. All's well. I decided what I needed was an adapter for that strange receptacle there in the wall. Probably there would be one downtown someplace. Maybe after a while I'd become accustomed to the Spanish bathroom. So they didn't have hot water. Cold did the job. I could reach little higher for the light switch and bend a little for the mirror and take a little noise from the john's thunder mug. But what I did need was an adapter. Something to bridge the gap between one source of power and another and make it all a little less frightening, even though shaving is a relatively simple task. Tomorrow I shall be prepared. There were no instructions with the toilet, but I guess I made it all right. But that poor spider really didn't have much of a chance to blend in. His fate led him down the drain.

10-12-65 Avenida de la Paz #16-2, Birthday

Morning of my 22nd birthday, I read Housman and Byron's poems—Housman made the most sense—then I wrote a poem. After lunch, I sat at my typewriter, watched traffic pass on Avenida de la Paz, and poured out memories on sheets of blue *Christoforo Colombo* stationary—memories of Columbus Day and my birthday always being celebrated together. At school, my second grade teacher Mrs. Strong, once told us the story of Christopher Columbus setting out for the New World on the *Nina*, *Pinta*, and *Sånta Maria*. They sailed off a flat world and fell forever into a dangerous dragon's underworld. The teacher acted out the fight between those dragons and Christopher to the tune of the "Star Spangled Banner," Columbus waving his Spanish passport and shouting: "Stay away from me, you nasty old dragon. Don't you bother me any more." Mrs Strong would laugh and stick out her tongue at the dragon, and we would laugh while Christopher went home crying to the king and queen, had apple pie for dessert, then went to bed. At home, my mother would come in from the kitchen carrying the cake with candles afire, everyone singing, stepfather turning off the lights, and in one great exhalation, I made a wish, then blew out the fire and light, and the world turned to smoke, smolder, and afterglow. After a moment, lights blazed again, my mother cut and served slabs of chocolate cake with scoops of ice cream and always my brother asked me about the wish I made. Usually I lied because I never made a wish.

10-12-65 Avenida de la Paz #16-2, The Underground Bar

"*Viva hombres, Viva Espana.*" Swaying room, frying shrimp, bocadillos, bread, back slaps, cigarette smoke, *chatos* of red wine. I found a corner in the taberna underneath the plaza, ordered a tinto. Never been there before but the underground cave's thick walls had an appeal. *Senor, vino y plata de cosas finas?* Low lights and smoke blurred my eyes, At the bar, a group of men slap, clap, chant *viva, viva, viva*, call out, hands raised over heads, the singer a half-drunk *gitano*, his wailing *cante hondo* coming through the smoke. Behind the bar, the weary sober white-aproned *camarero* washed, wiped, poured, joked, served, ready with his array of glasses to slake the thirst of the crowd for 23 cents a glass. The *gitano* sang again—half scream, half crying. A stranger in front of me put down his glass softly on the table. "Foreigner, there are women down the block waiting for you. There are women down the block." He panted over heavy tongue and oily jaws. One lone nude light bulb arching above us hung like the moon from a fly-spotted ceiling. I told them it was my birthday. I sang "*Cumple anos feliz...* They listened and clapped. The *gitano* listened. We exchanged songs. Salud. Salud. More toasts more *copas con gas*, Sebastian and Antonio came over. "Women? How many and what do they want?" I zipped up my jacket, looked up at his face, *Salud y viva las mujeres*. To the Virgin, salud to la Rioja. We stand up, the toast begins: *Por arriba, por abajo, por el centro, por adentro.* On the last phrase, we all drink together, glasses tipping up, throats cool with wine again, mouths wiped with hands, glasses diffuse nude light through the dregs, color the reddening beams overhead and on the hardwood table. *Camarero, tres mas copas con gas por favor.* Speaking in low voices, I don't know how long we waited there, huddled around the table together in the corner. The *gitano* and his *amigos* left, the cafe almost empty. Across the cold street and 50 meters straight up, the cathedral bells rang twice. Tuesday, October 12, I was a long way from home and knew it, and a long ways from being sober and didn't give a damn. Light headed, more drunk than I'd ever been, I said *muy buenas noches* to my companions, still asking where I was from, still toasting country, men, women, an endless circle of slang and smoke and good will. I stepped out into the cold night, started down the cobblestones in a slow steady stagger. At the *Plaza de Colon*, I stared up, gave a speech to the dark statue, remembered the local *dicho*: "A que indica Colon?/

la calle de pan y carbon." What does Columbus Point at? The street of bread and coal. At home, I tried to sleep, barfed all my wine to the floor. Mopped up with an undershirt. Slept.

10-13-65 Avenida de la Paz #16-2, University of Salamanca

Today I matriculated at the university, paid my tuition of $37 for the year. That leaves me with $400.00 and there should be $159 left in the bank. When I finish paying room and board at $2.00 per day, the money I have will be quite short. (Have to sell something back home.) Now up to my cerebellum in Spanish literature, language, history, and art. In all four classes, there was no time for questions or discussion, no syllabus, no Foreign Student advisor or group, no warm classrooms, no textbooks except in Spanish History. Loudspeakers crackled in and out, hard wooden seats, no coffee shop discussions with peers. Nevertheless, I listened , understood, took haphazard notes. Sat toward the back—behind all the other students.

10-15-65 Avenida de la Paz #16-2, Senora Teodora

The day I paid her my first rent, Senora Teodora was standing in the kitchen with a fork in her hand. A short, strong, middle-aged woman in a black dress and apron, she is broad-faced, toothless except for a small row along the lower jaw, and a voice that could sound harsh and loud then private and soft in the same minute. She wears thick black-rimmed glasses, and often comes out of the kitchen and peers at me through steamed lenses. Sometimes, she swears softly at the cat, says an ave, then rests her eyes silently on the white tiled walls and the decorative Disney tiles above the sink. The cat is in heat. Yowling and backing up to rub its ripe and frustrated body on the legs of chairs. "She's never been in the street," Teodoro explains. I have to remember to watch out for the cat sneaking out the door.

Every morning at the Sanchez apartment, I'm now used to waking in the dark to the bread man's cry, "*El panadero, el panadero,*" and lying in bed, I hear Senora Teodora unlock and unlatch the second-story apartment door. After an interval of silence, she descends the cold stairs, buys her round loaf of fresh bread, then ascends the four flights of stairs and latches the door again. At daylight, I hear her rattling the milk bucket as she ties a strong rope to the bail, then drops a few coins in the empty bucket and lowers it from her open window to the dairyman waiting below. He fills her bucket with two liters of fresh milk, attaches the tight telescoping lid, then gives the rope a jerk—his signal for her to start lifting. Standing at the open window and pulling hand over hand, Senora Teodora—with hefty shoulders and forearms—quietly raises the full bucket two stories. These two events start every day—breakfast is always *café con leche, pan y mantequilla.*

Senora Teodora orders the Sanchez family with grace, humor, intimidation, and strength. She showed me how to operate the Persian blinds—wooden slats that rose and fell outside my window. To heat the dining room and my room on these cold October nights, she prepares and places the round brazier pan of glowing charcoal, *un bracero,* beneath the table, so we can sit down, cover our lower bodies with the quilt draped over the table, and be warm—at least from the waist down. Humming and muttering, Senora Teodora cooked all the meals, scrubbed the red tiles of the kitchen floor, kept everyone happy.

Housewifery occupied the best hours of the day and night—cooking, cleaning, buying, selling, and more than once I have seen her thickly-muscled calves parallel with red tile at 9:00 pm as she swabbed the kitchen floor, humming and muttering to herself. Pillar of the house, authority on bigness of heart, superstitious, frugal, and over-weaningly maternal, Teodora managed not only the kitchen, but also the family, sustaining them in moments of death, shortage, and discord with wise counsel and short stories.

In fact, everyone depends on her calm strength of spirit to carry their lives along—wherever they are going. Husband Fulgencio depends on her listening ear, always an audience for his blustering, indignant reports of the day's gossip at the bank, and I've learned to look away when she shuts him up with a quick rebuff. Son Feliz is also dependent. If Teodora leaves the house, Feliz is without a listening ear and a doling hand, both of which are absolutely necessary for a 24-year old medical student. To her only son, Teodora is a soothing confessor and she finances his every whim. Her youngest daughter Luisa has attempted escape from Teodora's domain by taking a nursing course, but has recently returned home after failing to find a paying job. She gets teased about the cat. Her dependence is both maternal and financial. When Teodora is home, Luisa only has to do half of the housework, and bear half of the criticism by Fulgencio and Feliz. Some afternoons I meet Luisa all dressed up and strolling around the plaza with her girlfriends. She flashes her cheerful brown eyes and hopes her flattened nose might catch the eye of some romantically-inclined Spaniard. Going out for any possible occasion, Luisa also avoids the ravings of her father, especially when Don Fulgencio stays home on bank holidays and makes jokes and teases about the yowling horny cat, teasing designed to humiliate his single daughter without a *novio*. Luisa's face flushes red. I must look away. And of course, if Fulgencio sits at the dining room table and complains about anything, Teodora always explodes from the kitchen and comes to her daughter's aid, silencing Papa's cat joke with some sly, private crudity, or a squelch too vociferous for him even to remember what it was he was complained about. Luisa detests housework.

10-18-65 Avenida de la Paz #16-2

Warm October sun on sandstone this afternoon, I walked down *Avenida de la Paz* maybe 60-70 steps to the River Tormes. From my map I could see that two roads and bridges cross the river, one new and one ancient, one of stone, the other of steel, one 19 centuries old, the other perhaps 30 years. Both structures offer well-traveled routes into the city. The river was low, fallen leaves floated downstream. I loved the sound of the riffle, so I decided to cross the Tormes twice this afternoon.

Avoiding traffic, I first walked out on the steel bridge, the structure and the street *Avenida de la Paz Espanola* commemorating 27 years of Spanish peace that ended the *Guerra Civil*. Only cars are allowed to cross on the new steel bridge. No trucks. In the center of the four-lane roadbed, I jumped up and down, and the steel girders trembled with my 190 pounds. Any passing car made the suspended span vibrate. I leaned over the railing, watched the water flow toward Portugal, and as I crossed to the other side, the steel bridge seemed flimsy and would not bear the weight of time or maybe another Franco or *Guerra Civil*.

Walking back, I crossed the Tormes again, this time on the *Puente Romano*, as the Sanchez family told me. First built with granite during the reign of Roman emperors Augustus and Vespasian, the current bridge raised the road on 26 stone Roman arches. As I walked, the dusty one-way roadbed never moved an inch. A sign told truck drivers to use the Roman bridge if their load was over 16 tons. To see the river, I had to lean over the thick stone guard walls. Watching the water flow, I tried to imagine how many thousands of people had crossed here on their way to and from Salamanca. Now, I was one of them. At the entrance to the bridge, a huge stone sculpture of a headless bull stood on a pedestal facing the river. I wondered what that bull stood for, but no one at home knew the answer.

10-23-65 Avenida de la Paz #16-2

Took a long walk in the city today. It's a circular walled medieval city with the Tormes a natural defense and water supply. Wandered through crooked streets 8 or 10 feet wide, saw the escutcheons from past grandeur, the circular towers for defense converted into houses, other houses built on top of the wall, ancient hand-hewn hand-laid stones held together with new mortar. Every street in the old part of town is a museum and the churches are veritable textbooks of ancient architecture—so much I don't know, so much to learn.

I strolled around the arcade of the square central plaza which shaped the town—a four-sided 18th century sandstone masterpiece with a facade for each of the major social forces—church, university, national government, and local government. One on each side of the square. Very centralized, very solid, very crowded. Once the venue for bullfights, now the route for cars and busses belching black diesel smoke and roaring through the huge open doors of ancient arched gateways leading away from the plaza. In the arcades I passed all kinds of shops, looked in at the bakeries and bookstores, studied the men selling shoeshines and the blind man crying out his lottery tickets pinned to his coat. To locals, the plaza is a traditional place to *dar un paseo*, which means "take a walk or stroll."

I took a street leading away from the plaza, a tributary leading to still more stores, saw residences with bronze hands for knockers on thick doors carved in exquisite mahogany or oak. No one walks here so I went back to the plaza where I walked round and round again, trying to see if I could meet the same person twice, but I did not meet a familiar face again. Because of my history class, I recognized ethnic origins—dark brown eyes from the Moors, aquiline noses from Iberians and Goths and Jews, classic profiles from Rome, and everyone talking with the most articulate hands in the world. In the shelter of the arcade, you walk in and out like playing checkers, shuffle behind a farmer in his black beret who refuses to walk faster, then meet girls—four abreast, arms locked, marching and chanting. The frosted pastry looks good, but well, maybe, so I go inside and buy. After all, dinner won't be served until 10:30 and I'll be starving by then. Back in the strolling mainstream of humanity, I lick the sugar off both cheeks and fingers and taste the pastry again. As I pass the newsstand, I remember my lines from Chekhov's *The Seagull* where Dorn is praising Genoa, his favorite city in the world:

> Because of the crowds in the streets. Evenings, when you left your hotel, the entire street was full of people. You drift along with the crowd, no destination in mind, just back and forth; it becomes a living thing, and you become part of it, spiritually as well as physically; you begin to believe that a universal world soul is possible… like in your play, Konstantin, remember?

Out in the square, light rain starts falling, and a sea of umbrellas, mostly pastels, suddenly transform the arcade. I watch the restaurants fill with men who sit or stand—elbows on counters—glasses lifting and every time a door opens, I can smell coffee and food and smoke and wine. Leaning against the pillars of sandstone, men smoke and speak to each other in low tones. A couple all dressed up for some special occasion stare at me, the only foreign face and wearing a strange blue jacket. Most of them are probably on their way home after work, preoccupied with their world, following the trails between home and office and friends and markets.

Heading down a side street toward home, a lonely sign burns out its message: "*Ultramarinos.*" I don't know what this means. Yesterday after noon I saw men scrubbing that same spot with a wire brush. The sign says, "Here is where a woman died." Here comes a girl I've seen before. "*Hola, buenas noches.*" That's all? I get a passing wave. She's obviously on her way somewhere, so I walk on, changing hands from pants pockets to coat pockets, keeping up my slow pace, catching snatches of conversation. As I amble by, people never know I'm eavesdropping. Behind me, down a dark street and out of this labyrinth, I think of Theseus and his unwinding string and the Minotaur killed long ago.

Passing the Torre del Clavero, a round medieval fortress with crossbow and rifle slits from the ground up, the lights and shadows begin to blend into chocolate and yellow marble mixed together by the spoon of the rising moon. I pass the *Guardia Civil* quarters, loud voices converse behind a wall, higher and softer women's voices float down from a dimly lighted second story window. Their words come dancing out on the balcony between the overhanging flowers, catch on wrought iron, then fall to me on the sidewalk. I hear singing in the Catholic Church next to the *quartel*. Yes, must be Sunday. That's why singing—something classical, probably Mass. I put an ear to the door. The art of arts I learned to appreciate; it gives the soul expression beyond the rational, a foreign language to the mind, but music makes its appeal to the ears and our response tells us more than we know about ourselves as beings more emotional than rational. Escaping from the stares of two old women dressed in black veils, black coats, black stocking and black shoes (Chekhov might say they were in mourning for their lives.) I walked off again toward home taking a series of dark shadowy cobblestone side streets. Finally arrived at *16 Segundo*. It was 10:20. Senora Teodora and Luisa were cooking dinner on the gas stove in the kitchen. Senor Fulgencio took out his pocket knife and cut wedges of the fresh bread for everyone. Soup, bread, water, eggs, or tortilla or fish, then hot milk or fruit. At 11:00 at night—delicious.

10-29-65 Avenida de la Paz #16-2

Rented a bike this morning. Crossed the Tormes on the steel bridge, rode rattling along the row of gold shimmering poplars reflected in the river until I reached the Roman bridge. At the intersection, one sign pointed to "Avila," the other said "Portugal." I chose Portugal. That's where Jacqueline lived, the girl from the boat, and it might be a better road. As I sat the hard seat and pedaled slowly, my wheels bounced over the cobblestones set on edge in the dirt. Here and there, spectators and other riders, but no one in a hurry. I passed a mule cart, a scooter whizzed past, and in his exhaust I saw his back—nothing more. I passed white-washed brick houses with red tile roofs. Odors jumped out like flagmen waving me down: roasting chestnuts, sweaty horses, manured cows, drying sausage, green wood smoke, salted meat, dead fish, eucalyptus, sour garbage. It was like passing through ten or twenty different kitchens and barn yards at once. At some of the odors I lifted my head and smiled, at others I bowed my head, held my breath, pedaled harder, as though I were escaping from the jaws of a pursuing dog. There were dogs, too—brown, skinny, dirty. They lay beside the road in the sunny dust panting easily, heads erect, while flies buzzed around their heads like electrons cycling around a nucleus. (These were not the sleek lank greyhounds I had seen with rabbit hunters in town.) Pedaling down the road toward Portugal, I sang my old songs. I knew no songs from here.

Riding out of town, gently rolling slopes caught the bike wheels and sent me flying downhill to a creek bottom where a magpie—good old magpies—sat black and white and blue in the morning sun. A sparrow sang, a brown swallow flitted by, and no longer was I a stranger. Lined with poplars, the road stretched out like a red typing ribbon over the humps of a pillow, rising easily at the next hill. Pedaling uphill was a bit sweaty, but nothing any worse than climbing Cornwall Avenue in Bellingham which I used to fly down by streetlights each morning delivering the *Seattle PI*. Up, up, rhythmically, round, round, I stood up and pumped the pedals and the sprocket and chain whirled around around as I pulled on the handlebars of the Spanish bicycle and sailed over the crest of one Castilian hill and rolled down the next hill into another swale.

Red dirt fields lined both sides of the *camino* to Portugal now, their color the same as the fields of Carolina and Virginia I had seen from the Greyhound window two years earlier when returning from Ecuador. Then another familiar picture came tumbling out of my memory—sunset and smoke and Scarlet's crying face as she walked over the burned fields of Tara—then I was gone down the road again to the first little town—Doninos—that had grown up there out of the red clay. As I cycled through, a few clucking red hens greeted me, and one small brown face peeked around a gate, bright eyes staring at me, his brown body completely naked. I winked; he disappeared. A quiet Saturday morning in Doninos. When I saw a woman scrubbing her new sidewalk, I called out *"Buenas dias"* and she replied with a silent quizzical stare. So, I called to her again and she finally cracked a grin, and I rode out of town into the fields again feeling close to wind and birds and men and women—anyone who had this dirt beneath their nails and in their skins and shoes.

A flock of merino sheep filled the road, so I followed their tinkling bells a while; their grazing sounded like a thousand wind chimes quaking. The sheep's dumb and dutiful faces were familiar to me and their backs made me think of the wool sweater I wore. Stopped and straddling the bike, I watched as one ewe moved slowly into another's grazing territory, bringing a head butt from the owner. By then the shepherd with his black beret had sized me up, so I raised my right hand to him to which he immediately replied by pointing his staff straight up to the sky. I took that for exuberance and rode around the sheep to the next horizon.

From my vantage point on the road, another sloping valley spread before me. Realizing how far I had come—at least 7 or 8 miles—I didn't want to go further. Every inch of that road would have to be retread so, deciding to turn around, I leaned the bike against a handy rock and climbed to the top of the roadcut.

Red clay fields spread before me again, but their lines were broken now by a farmer walking behind a team of mules pulling a plow. He walked back and forth, one hand on the plow, one on the reins. Somehow he also carried a stick. At the end of each row, the mules would stop, he would juggle the reins and stick, shout something that sounded like "Moo-la," and the mule team would pivot on their back hooves, turn, and start down the next furrow, the farmer stepping behind them in perfect synchronicity. As I sat there staring at this Spanish peasant farmer who still worked the earth with animals instead of machines, I could hear the creak and rub of the leather harness. My grandfather would have had something to say to him, but what could I say.

Suddenly, behind me, a tractor back-fired and started. I turned to the familiar noise. Black diesel smoke boiled toward the sky and the tractor rolled down the field. After a moment, I turned back to the plowman and his mules. I wondered if he wondered about me, because I knew he had seen me when I pedaled up the hill. I would always remember him but probably he would never know who I was or that a wandering boy from America had watched him plow that morning there in his red clay field on the Spanish meseta beside the highway to Portugal. When his furrows came closer and closer to me, I turned, scrabbled down the bank, turned my bike, and rode back to Salamanca.

4.
Salamanca Fall
November
1965

UPPER LEFT:
Business card greeting

CENTER:
Salamanca City Map

LOWER LEFT:
Ink dot is Avenida de la Paz residence

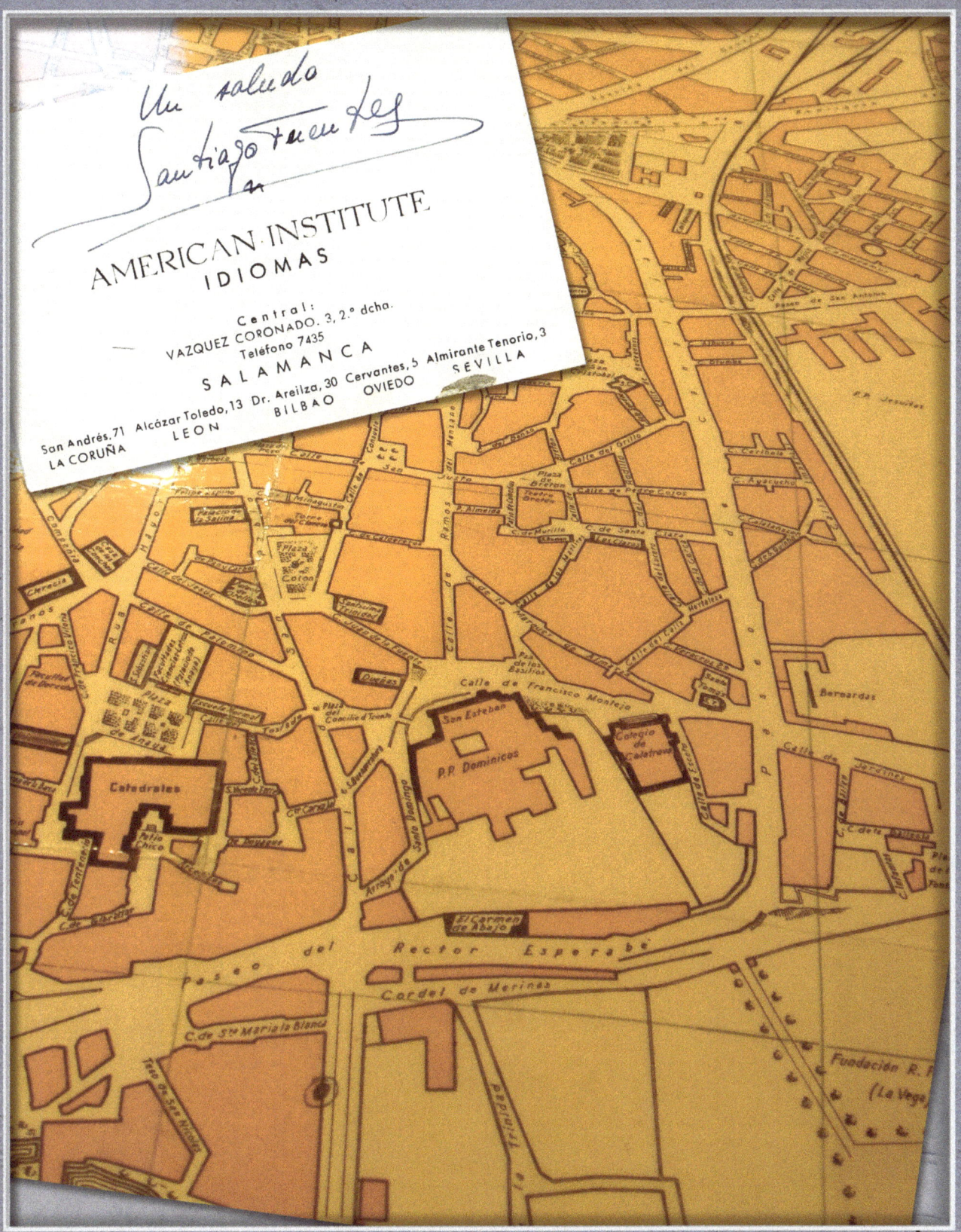

11-1-65 Avenida de la Paz #16-2, Expelled

Got expelled from the famous university today. No more stuffed-shirt boring monologues for me. No more cold classroom, no more being the only foreign student in the room. Wasn't paying any attention when Professor Somebody called me to the front of the class, told me not to come back until I had better manners. I didn't care. I'm tired of being a student. Spanish classmates I never knew stared as I got the hell out of there, ran down the stone stairs, out the doors, into the cold and welcome street. Bought a chocolate bar with *almendras*, walked slowly to the Plaza Mayor. Inside the farmer's café, I ordered tea with lemon to calm down and get warm, then just sat and wrote notes about street life for a couple hours, stared out the window once in a while at the fubsy housewives in black coats and tight scarves shopping and passing by while indoors I took in—again—the farmers' soft black jackets and black berets, cigarette smoke, clatter of dishes, stolid ancient faces. My academic cover story, the "Junior Year Abroad," turns out to be a fiction I'd invented to justify my desire to explore. To the famous university of Salamanca I will never go back. I'm going to hit the road, find people and places I'd already missed: kids playing street soccer, women bickering over onions, Vespa scooters whizzing past, boys *toreando* passing cars like bullfighters, black jackdaws circling the cathedral, students ignoring the bust of Unamuno the Loco, fishwives whacking gleaming fins and heads and tails on marble counters, old *castanara* huddling over her brazier of roasting chestnuts, chess masters playing without looking at the board at the *ateneo*, farmers in black berets drinking wine in the cafés, black/white nuns walking arm in arm, gypsies wailing *cante hondo* in the bars, street musicians *tocando* taut guitars under balcony windows, sandstone buildings glowing gold at sunset, vendors selling hot-roasted peanuts in the shell, children in the park teaching me the Spanish words for *swan*, *goose*, and *duck*.

11-8-65 Avenida de la Paz #16-2

Today a cold wind blows from León southward to La Mancha, a penetrating relentless cold of many winters in Castile. People unconsciously fight their collars, lean headlong, faces ruddy, burned, cold, eyes watering in rivulets of pain down cheeks too old to crease any more. This is an unmerciful cold that comes running down the Cantabrians, mounts the Sierra de Gredos, slams into the Guadarrama, cuts the land in two, a keen, sharp, and spine-shaking blow, an incision to essence. An old woman selling roasted chestnuts huddles next to her charcoal brazier, her sharp knife whittling the hard cover, opening the hard meat, soon to be roasted, soft, hot, and ready for eager hands. I saw children buy those roasted chestnuts just to warm their cold red hands then, when their hands were warm, they peeled and ate the remaining heat. I saw the blind lottery sellers in the plaza, men and women unable to see the world, selling in begging commands, intoned deep baritone and alto. Their chants fill the murmuring crowd, white canes tap the stones, then gusts of dusty, rusty, cutting wind blow their voices away. Women, blind and goitered, squat near an arch or a pillar for protection, shivering faces, freezing feet, but selling, selling, selling. Barter and buy for life, sell your soul for heat, fire, home, escape, escape, escape, then return tomorrow to sell again. The wind will be waiting. It blows night and day while the Tormes creeps silently to the sea. Now, the poplars by the river stand naked against the leaden silver sky, stripped and left helpless, their children of a season fallen and blown away or rotting near their roots. People hide their hands in pockets of fur-collared coats of the country. Black berets lower their summer's cocky tilt, now hide ears instead of showing hair. Once learned, the lesson of winter never leaves. Here, the names of months end with "e" that in English end with "ber." They all bring back blowing snow and the laughing death of nordic hell and man freezing—a helpless smile, a cold unremembered death among the snow-white beds of Hospital Provincial.

11-14-65 Avenida de la Paz #16-2

Dear Mom, Dad, Dave and Shorty:

It is with visions of Idaho tamarack and pine mixed in a foggy gold and green that I sit here behind this machine in Spain looking out on a windy day in Castile. Here, the first tired leaves are falling along the Tormes while daily the clouds multiply as they slide across the sky from the Portuguese coast. There, I am sure the rusty, dusty, musty fall has also fallen along the path through the park in Spirit Lake, early mornings find nude bushes bearded in white, and any day now it might snow on Mt. Spokane. It is now, away from all that personal history, that I understand the lines from Wordsworth: "the child is father of the man." Too many hours of cradling the .270 while walking, stalking on beds of quiet needles, too many nights of crackling fireplace conversation, and too many days of following footprints in the snow will contribute to a return and to a renewed appreciation of the west Columbus never saw.

You might be led to believe that it is homesickness, or a pungent nostalgia that causes thoughts like the preceding to flow from this mind that you know, but I can assure you it is not. It is rather the beginning of awareness, awareness of what my own mind contains, awareness of the strength of environment, and awareness of the nobility of patriotic sentiment(which I have often degraded because of its results and anti-Christian ideals). It is also the beginning of realization that men are basically creatures of a small part of the globe because of the inescapable nature of environmental influence, and the universal nature of local sentiment, feeling for one's surroundings. For it is with great hesitation that I personally would leave the Northwest now, unless I were assured that it was there, before a roaring fire in December, I could spend the winter of my days on earth. Every man is attached, of that there is no doubt, and only unbearable circumstances or extraordinary influences will serve to remove him distantly from what his eyes have seen, his ears heard, and his feet walked upon since the day he learned to appreciate and experience the physical world.

And not only are men attached, they are passionately attached. If asked why they like the desert, most will reply, "Because I like it." These circular arguments would be laughed out of logic class, but to those who are close to the earth and feel its pulse beneath their feet, and its heart beating at sunset, it is the most logical answer. Why?

Because it is seldom that words can lift out of the mind what lies close to the heart. It is seldom that men have the occasion or the desire or the ability to express what they experience as meaningful in life. A stammer, a great inhaling or exhaling, a rounding of the mouth, or just plain speechlessness usually characterizes man's reaction to grandeur, to beauty, to love, to pain, or to any emotionally based, passionate experience.

So it is the task of the man who has chosen to attempt to catch in words a passing moment, the essence of its beauty or its life, to understand the beings that feel the presence of something greater than themselves. It is no common task to attempt such a circumscription, and a less common event to succeed in the same.

So it is that I have finally made some sort of occupational statement, one long incoming and far-reaching in ramifications. And it is because of that statement that I am now seriously considering calumniating study at the University of Salamanca in order to go a traveling with a pack sack on my back, along the roads of Spain, Italy, and Greece between now and the time when I shall return to the College of Idaho; that being tentatively September of the year that comes around the corner in December. However unreasonable that sort of transient desire may be, it is directly in line with all that has been said above; for if men are to be understood, they must be seen in context, like bees in a hive or in flight, not in the biology book where all their buzzing and stinging and dizzy aerial antics are gone. It is a matter of placement. Either to first prepare the mind and then eat the food of experience, risking stereotyped ideas, preconceived opinions, prejudice and excessive subjectivity, or using that knowledge and energy to prepare the mind, thereby avoiding pedantry, intolerance, ignorance of a special type, and other such hobgoblins that often haunt the dead curiosity.

Not only is the life on the road broadening, enriching, and educational, it also serves as a talisman of confidence and faith. It is the challenge of going into circumstances completely foreign, and making your appeal on the basis of your humanity, and that only, that provides the instruction. For then you discover what really are the basic allegiances of men, what their concerns are, and how they live in context. Like the beekeeper opening the hive I would like to be, but also like one bee searching into all the world I shall be. Byron said it was "the passion and the power to roam." It is an escape from the ordered way, the day by day routine between doors, into an unordered way, an unpredictable way, a meal to meal routine, a town to town routine, with the environment constantly changing history all around, salted and peppered with humanity. Can you, leaving all the environment behind that you have ever known, go out into the world and follow your curiosity, wherever it might lead? It is commitment to the yes or no of that question that now faces me. For it will not be forever that I shall be able to follow my curiosity, as a child follows a rolling ball, nor will I ever be able to catch my curiosity, but neither will I be able to escape it. To know, to see, to feel, to speak, to eat; these and uncountable number of other reasons will lead me down the road, an inconspicious figure, an anonymous walker, a special traveler, asking only to remain inconspicuous, unnamed, and free to converse with any man beside his fire. No, I shall not spend 40 years in the wilderness, but I have already spent 22 years in Egypt. No, I do intend to escape this great cloud of security and euphoria that is now surrounding me.

    If I sound convinced, I am. I am convinced, I should sound that way.

11-14-65 Avenida de la Paz #16-2, Busqueda del Tesoro

Today was rain. A shifting, sifting, drifting, lifting mist that covered the sun when it tried to climb over the horizon. Thousands of particles fell on the alfalfa, trees, and grass in the convent garden across the street. Few people in the streets at 9:00 when Feliz Huerta and I came down to the wet and slippery sidewalk, strode forward together in the rain. There was just enough to wet the face, like heavy coastal fog that drops like tons of cotton candy wool on Tacoma and Seattle. More fog, more rain. Dirty rivulets floated orange peels, cigarette butts, and chestnut hulls, carried them to the storm drain, then runoff water fell through the grate to the dark echoing underground. Below the sidewalk the gutters were also starting to flow, hesitating around high spots in the cobblestones and running wild across some declivities where gravity has favored them with slowing down. Turning the corner, Feliz met and spidered into a waiting car. I waved, and they were off to rendevous with the students of the Faculty of Medicine where Feliz was a student. They were sponsoring the treasure hunt by auto. At 10:00 I joined them and other cars in the plaza for the start of the race, thinking it might be an interesting spectacle because cars are second-generation here. Standing there in the mist, hands pocketed and head hooded, watching the water bead off my beautiful blue coat, "Hey," someone called, and I got in a VW bug with two Spaniards and driver Pamela Bond—a good looking Canadian woman my age, a miniature Cleopatra looking for an Anthony by the Tormes. Riding in her VW—a gliding barge—we left the plaza and spent the madcap morning and three hours of the drizzling afternoon driving the rainy cobblestones searching for a list of ridiculous objects to gather before anyone else, a kind of hide-and-seek because one of the objects and stations was mobile. All shifts and turns, stop and go, turn and brake, honk and wave, watch out, wipers slapping, not here, over there, you go, we'll go, where to, how long, what time, 0K and why, where the snails? no snails? no, where snails? Bar Munoz snails? Yes and now, here and here, cathedrals and puzzles, pajamas and frogs, flies and cats, how many for St. Ives? your house or mine, where and when, "Nice meeting you." Best moment of the day—Pamela invited me to visit her in Paris. Home at 3:15 for a Saint's Day party for Sr. Fulgencio. (Custom to celebrate the saint's day as birthday.) Didn't ask who his patron saint was. He taught me an ironic *dicho* about walking: Question: "*Como has venido?*" Answer: "*En el coche de San Fernando. Unos veces a pie, otros andando.*" Feast of spaghetti, roast stuffed with peas, olives, peppers, pastry, fried potatoes, that's it. A short siesta, then wrote a long letter to Philip LeClaire, my Spirit Lake neighbor. So much nostalgia for neighborhood kids to share and remember. The typewriter clicked and clacked away—two full pages single-space.

11-16-65 Avenida de la Paz #16-2, Alice Letter

Today, this surprise love letter came from Alder. Oh, my beautiful blonde Alice! My secret passion has found me. Rescued me. Tears flooded my eyes. I convulsed, bent, cried. Read her blue words again and again. Never received anything like this. Copied it here to read over and over.

November 16,1965

Hello my Darling—

I saw your address in the paper and couldn't resist. Just as other instances concerning you, I find it very difficult to deny myself an opportunity to communicate with you. I am, however, limiting myself to this one letter, so Merry Christmas, dear. This is my gift to you—so small and yet I hope it is received in the light that it is given.

We have seen each other so little, and I know very little about you and yet I feel I know you well. I have infinite trust that your intentions are true. From the first day at Alder, you struck me as something very special and you have been in my thoughts since that time. Just knowing you briefly has changed my outlook on life immeasurably. It has given me something of my own to dream about, and because I am an incurable romantic and dreamer, I suppose I thrive on this.

You have also become a magnificent obsession to me, just as a child with a new toy who has been forbidden to play with it. I love your beautiful words and because they are few and far between all are cherished, pondered on lovingly and remembered in detail. Thank you, darling, for a lovely dream. I wouldn't trade our lovely beautiful hours nor do I regret them. I find ways to justify them to myself and also to ease an over active conscience.

Along with being a dreamer, I am also quite realistic, believe it or not. I have learned (not easily) to accept my life as it is and to be thankful for it, because it is a good life. I could not ask for any more and I am very grateful to my adopted family for what they have done for me.

To return to a lighter side of this picture, I visited our special place on your birthday and the day you were to arrive at your destination and you didn't seem quite so far away.

I walked along the beach for a few moments and even found another small stone to throw in for luck. The day was dreary and rather sad. At any rate, speaking of birthdays, it occurred to me that we are 2 years and 4 months apart in age instead of 3. I was 25 the last day of May. Something rather insignificant and yet it made me feel a little better. I dislike being the "one who should know better."

I must close now and perhaps we can wave at each from our pedestals.

Joys of love are but a moment long
Pain of love endures a whole life long

Your eyes kissed mine,
I saw the love in them shine
You brought me heaven right there
While your eyes kissed mine

My love loves me
and all the wonders I see
A rainbow shines in my window,
My love loves me

And now he's gone,
like a dream that fades into dawn
But the words stay locked in my heart strings
My love loves me.

The words to this lovely song seem to fit nicely but there are many that do. In one of my lonelier moments in Tennessee, I even composed a poem, and since I know absolutely nothing about poetry, you can imagine what it was like. At least it has feeling!

God go with you my love,

Alice

11-20-65 Avenida de la Paz #16-2, Interview Santiago

After abandoning the famous University of Salamanca, I sought out a part-time job teaching English at the American Institute, a private language school owned and operated by the Spanish linguist Santiago Fuentes—middle-aged, bristling red mustache, competent English, impeccable suits and neat bow ties. In my job interview, Senor Fuentes approved my northwest American accent and added me to his cadre of five young emigre teachers. (For good reason, I would meet them later.) Because I'd taught Ecuadorians for the U.S. Information Agency in Quito for a year, I felt experienced (though actually still an ESL apprentice) and I delighted in my new English students: a class of Spanish Air Force pilots wanting to better communicate with their U.S. counterparts; a tutorial for a Puerto Rican couple—Juan and Miriam Cruz—headed for the United States after Juan finished medical school; a class of bright 8th grade girls and boys. Unlike my own abandoned classes at the famous University, these classes at the American Institute were small, the students friendly, the text books plentiful, the classrooms warm. Getting paid for teaching there twenty-four hours a week became a kind of bonus and refuge. And after late class some November afternoons, Senor Fuentes would invite me for coffee and a game of chess at the Ateneo. His booming language institute business made him friendly, but if I outsmarted Senor Fuentes in an end game of pawns and rooks, he always huffed and steamed and demanded we play one more game.

11-21-65 Avenida de la Paz #16-2, Winter Snow Comes

This morning I lifted my eyes to the Sierra and found them covered with new snow. Come in the night without warning, snow dropped a woolly white blanket of cold over the landscape, snow brought metamorphosis, snow changed a brown and dying hillside to the white of new life, far removed, distant, yet snow came close to the contours of earth. Its forms are as the daily clouds–changeable, multiple, and various. Some days the drifting powder will race along over a crusted surface, like a knife whetting its edge on ice; other days it floats down in heavy, suspended flakes, filling the infinite air with a white kaleidoscope of uncountable feathers dropping silently to a common bed; yet other days find snow dejected, sad, weeping, sagging when the collected dirt from surrounding chimneys stains and filters down slowly through the crevasses that time and a clear sun have caused. If snow remains through a night when the air drops below that critical point at which things die, you may see it the following morning glistening, sparkling, in granules of diamond splendor, bordering most any muddy puddle or sidewalk, and if the rising sun focuses its all-consuming light on those common unnumbered jewels, they become fading prisms leaving the earth in their solidity to return to rivulets, gutters, streams, lakes, rivers, oceans, and all their beauty will be lost in the change of nature. Yet snow is not without hope, for hope is everpresent as the flitting bird through underbrush in a forest: heard as it chirps from branch to twig, but never seen and seldom captured, even by the most diligent of hunters. Some day, as the land breeze begins to blow, catching the surging ocean unaware in its blue obsidian wave crests, that skiff of snow may return to fall again and once again the water that ran down the rivulets in melting sadness rises in triumph, rides over a coastal plain, sweeps up the mountainside, rising on air, then the burden of clouds is once again dropped to the waiting earth. Without warning snow has come again, and in the rapture of momentary beauty, of unseen wonder, it falls, but falling is not its end. For nature reveals its soul to be circular, infinite, beyond the pale in the vale of origins, secrets untold, and thoughts unspoken, phenomena unobservable. Who can measure himself beside snow?

5.
Salamanca Winter
December
1965

UPPER LEFT:
intro, teacher strike text

LOWER LEFT:
pocket calendar of
American Institute, '65

CENTER:
signed Christmas card
from students
(background is text
of teacher strike)

LOWER RIGHT:
front of Christmas card
from students
(background is continued text
of teacher strike)

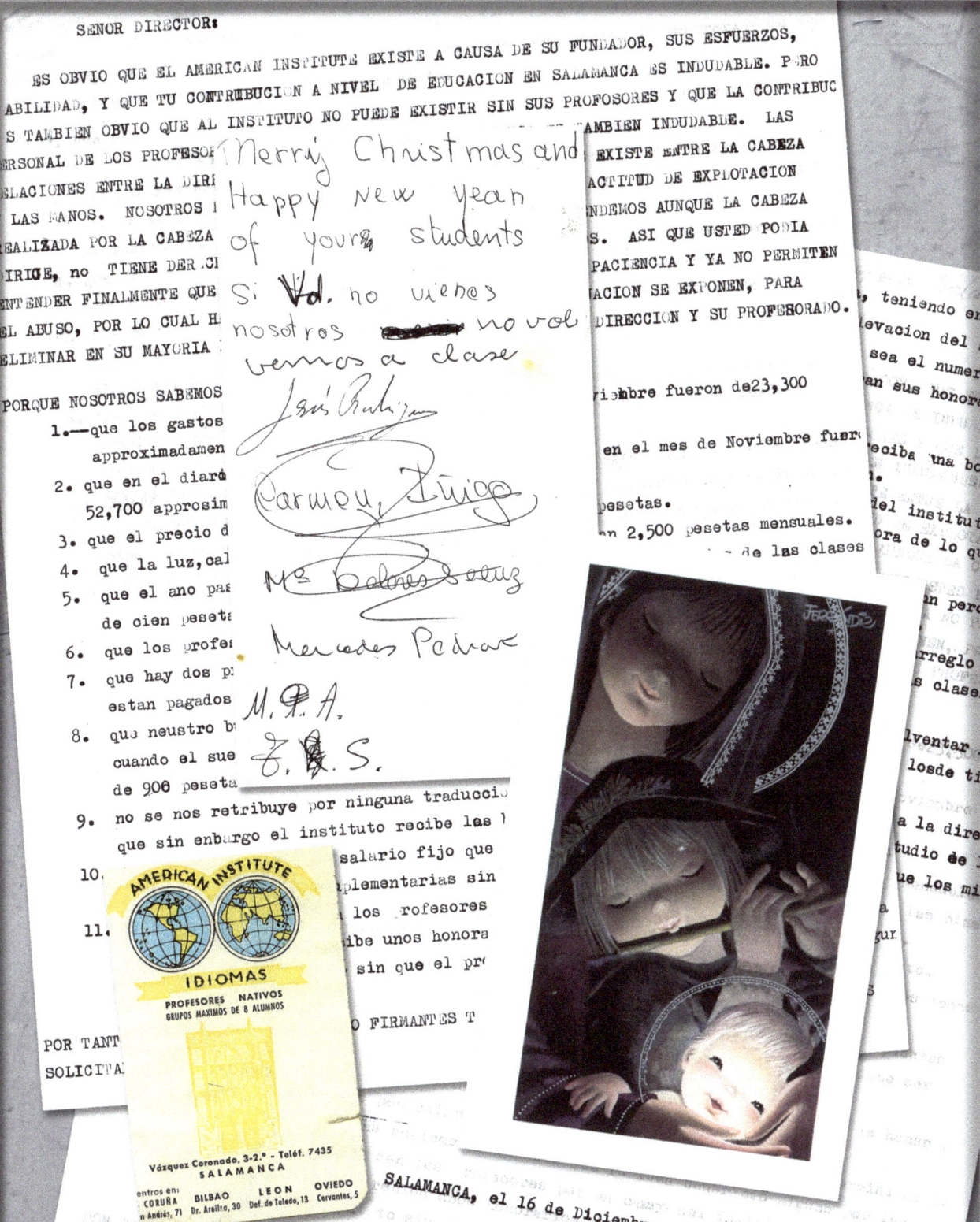

SEÑOR DIRECTOR:

ES OBVIO QUE EL AMERICAN INSTITUTE EXISTE A CAUSA DE SU FUNDADOR, SUS ESFUERZOS, ...ABILIDAD, Y QUE TU CONTRIBUCION A NIVEL DE EDUCACION EN SALAMANCA ES INDUDABLE. PERO ...S TAMBIEN OBVIO QUE AL INSTITUTO NO PUEDE EXISTIR SIN SUS PROFESORES Y QUE LA CONTRIBUC... ...ERSONAL DE LOS PROFESOR... ...TAMBIEN INDUDABLE. LAS ...ELACIONES ENTRE LA DIR... ...EXISTE ENTRE LA CABEZA ...Y LAS MANOS. NOSOTROS ... ...ACTITUD DE EXPLOTACION ...REALIZADA POR LA CABEZA ... ...ENDEMOS AUNQUE LA CABEZA ...DIRIGE, no TIENE DER.C... ...S. ASI QUE USTED PODIA ...ENTENDER FINALMENTE QUE ... ...PACIENCIA Y YA NO PERMITEN ...EL ABUSO, POR LO CUAL H... ...ACION SE EXPONEN, PARA ...ELIMINAR EN SU MAYORIA ... ...DIRECCION Y SU PROFESORADO.

PORQUE NOSOTROS SABEMOS...

1.— que los gastos ... approximadamen...
2. que en el diar... 52,700 approxim...
3. que el precio d...
4. que la luz, cal...
5. que el año pas... de cien peseta...
6. que los profe...
7. que hay dos p... estan pagados...
8. que nuestro b... cuando el sue... de 900 peseta...
9. no se nos retribuye por ninguna traduccio... que sin enbargo el instituto recibe las ...
10. ... salario fijo que ... ...plementarias sin ... los ... rofesores
11. ... ibe unos honora... ...sin que el pr...

POR TANT...
SOLICITA...

...iembre fueron de 23,300
... en el mes de Noviembre fuer...
... pesetas.
... 2,500 pesetas mensuales.
...— de las clases

... FIRMANTES T...

SALAMANCA, el 16 de Diciembre de 1965.

Merry Christmas and Happy New Year of yours students

Si Vd. no vienes nosotros no volvemos a clase

Jesús Rodríguez
Carmen Zúñiga
Mª Dolores ...
Mercedes Pedra...
M.P.A.
...S.

AMERICAN INSTITUTE
IDIOMAS
PROFESORES NATIVOS
GRUPOS MAXIMOS DE 8 ALUMNOS

Vázquez Coronado, 3-2º - Teléf. 7435
SALAMANCA

Centros en: CORUÑA BILBAO LEON OVIEDO
...Andrés, 71 Dr. Areilza, 30 Def. de Toledo, 13 Cervantes, 5

12-1-65 Avenida de la Paz #16-2

Dear Mom, Dad, Dave, Carol, and et al,

I'm still thinking that the "and" in that greeting is unnecessary but, being too lazy to change it, or if you like another point of view thinking it a great error, I left it as it is. Having not heard from you for some time, I decided to send another short carrier pigeon across the Atlantic with news, thoughts, and requests, hoping that he might be sent back with news that the flood had abated and we can now safely land on Ararat.

Of the 168 hours in the week, my time is now spent in the following amounts: 64 hours of sleep (wherein is much loss). 24 hours of teaching English (wherein much gain)... 2 eating (wherein is more loss than gained), and the other 47 may be spent in any number of ways. No, I have not forgotten God. The main preoccupations now are the future, ways to live it, how to prepare for it, and how not to waste the present, the main occupations are reading, writing, speaking, and teaching. (The present participle there indicates not only action but also a state of being.) Yesterday I was paid by the American Institute for teaching, speaking pays everyday but in less obvious tender; writing's salary is latent, unknown, but realized and appreciated more by the soul than by the pocket; while reading's remuneration immeasurable, as Francis Bacon has pointed out. I am consequently a rich man, although I own little, hold title to nothing, and have invested only myself and time in some unseen future enterprise that will pay in satisfaction and healthy retrospection, a sense of contribution to society, and a full-realization of my potentialities, if they can be spoken of in the plural.

The last letter remains, for me, still a mystery in several ways, and yet it is full of ideas that I have long entertained and longer still examined. However, they have been confined somewhat since that writing, for now I am not going to cold Italy, Greece, or the Egyptian halls or sand and pharaohs, but rather will expend the majority of the moments of light in southern Spain until the spring. I have decided that because a bee of value judgment came and stung me into believing that it would be better to know the history and life of one part well than just to have seen but not understood many parts. You don't suppose this is the beginning of specialization? If it is, I still don't feel very specialized.

Any addresses of people here on the continent will probably be more than useful when the feathered tribe flies north and I go with them. Let's not go too deep into the barrel however, for it might be a bit disconcerting if, after knocking on door somewhere, some place, some time I had to explain for half an hour who I was and what that should mean to them. Even hospitality can be overtaxed here, although some would have you believe otherwise.

Rather than send the US NEWS AND WORLD REPORT to a traveling dilettante who may not have an address after the first of January, why don't you send him some newly discovered necessities for travel? I unquestionably need a one man pup tent, light, waterproof with a floor. One can be purchased here for $33, but I have the thought that something made in the States will be lighter, more durable, and much more satisfactory. I can also use a can of that water proofing boot grease or wax or whatever it is to use on my heavy shoes. Small plastic containers and plastic sacks would also be a great help. If you can find these things and it doesn't cost a fortune to send them, print the word REGALO which means gift on the outside and no one will open it. If the pup tent is too expensive for a gift, take some money out of my account to pay for it because without it I am lost. Also, if you can find a sheet of heavy plastic that will fit beneath the tent as a ground cloth, it would serve well. The rest of the equipage I can find here, or already have. They sell little bottles of gas with a burner top that can be carried in a pack sack easily and last for 20 hours at least. Once the bottle(which is metal) is purchased, the cost of the gas is negligible. I can live easily for 40 to 50 pesetas a day, which amounts to about .80 cents a day, eating well and cooking my own food. It will sort of be an extended Mt. Rainier trip, Dad, or camping on the Olympic peninsula in miniature. Not an easy life, but with the harmonica, imagination, a book or two, and new country to see and people with which to speak, it should be an enriching, enlightening, and educational experience, however informal.

I was reminded the other day of the song "Duna" that has circulated among the lyrically inclined in our family and while thinking about the lyrics I thought how, in a certain sense, they are quite fitting. Another that comes to mind Dougie sang for the spring festival in Coeur d' Alene is "The Vagabond." I can still see him on that little stage in the NIJC south wing belting out those last notes while Dad's head moved between the keys and the stage as he kept Doug in time or kept in time with Doug on those last notes. Then there is Gramp's hand with the crooked little finger that suddenly swings up and starts to keep time as the round, cavernous mouth opens, the eyes sparkle, the face reddens through a small rustle of whiskers, and "I tramp the road, the long wide road, over mountain, sea, and plain," comes rumbling, rolling, in smooth and heavy tones, from registers too deep and too unknown to explore. Funny, I never really did sing that song. Perhaps I was predestined to live it. Let's not drop into the metaphysical just now though because it's really too heavy for this context.

Martin Cane looks as British as Winston Churchill without his cigar. He was trained for the priesthood, never went to university, and comes from a district in the English moorland just west of Wuthering Heights. How he happened to turn up in Salamanca with his blonde hair and blue eyes, slight stature and brown suitcase is somewhat unknown. But he walks the streets daily, lives in a pension, suffers through some of the more extemporaneous Spanish meals, and spends a good deal of his time at the American Institute. There, by choice and necessity, he teaches the real English language to able students, tolerates the unable students, and keeps up a constant British chatter in the halls between classes. He's 28, and still realizing the other side of life that devout Catholicism classes categorically as sinful. As you might have guessed, Martin and I have kindled a friendship that may burn significantly in my future and his, for he once hibernated in a little French fishing village and tried to write for money. It proved unsuccessful. To date, we have spent long hours of, the morning and wee hours of night chatting, as he titles it, about a variety of topics. They may range from the catholic cosmology, to the influence of the Bible on western literature, to London, to the west land where there is a horizon that can still be unmarred by beer-cans and telephone poles. A man interested in history, uninterested in pedantry, and disinterested in nothing: we have much in common. It is amazing how many brothers the world contains, and still more amazing how few we bother to know.

So, for this time, I shall shut up, with a Merry December when it's time to remember, think of your brother. and then of another, and others will follow like migrating swallow, to south, away from the mouth of the sharpened wind of Castile.

Some protein pills would help. Send a recipe for apple pie. I've forgotten how to make the crust. That's a bad sentence. I've forgotten the ingredients for the crust, but do remember the rest, With the exception of the baking time. Today I'm making a banana, grape, strawberry jello dessert for the household who have never tasted it before. The way to a country's heart is through its stomach, until its stomach gets big, and then they have a hard time seeing their heart, or where the bigness of stomach came from.

12-7-65 Avenida de la Paz #16-2, Letters

Got 4 letters in one day: Sanders, Mayos, Mom, Louie Attebery. He sent campus news–first in a long time. Filled me in on the Nelson Rockefeller visit. Admires him. He's rich and smart and smooth. Made all the local wealthy happy. Starting the new library. No mention of my letters to him. Probably too busy teaching and keeping his wife and kids happy. He and Boles been bird hunting—sage grouse and pheasants. Boles got a big grouse, he said. Louie didn't go deer hunting, but he did buy a new Browning .22 (auto) for blue grouse but never saw any birds all day. Did some plinking. Reminded me of Spirit Lake and hunting on Mt. Hoodoo with Fred Shaw and watching him shoot the head off a blue grouse perched on a pine limb 100 yards away. That .243 had a good scope. Makes me think of hunting with my .270 and walking on the gold tamarack needles west of town. Got my first deer there. Across the street I sometimes see a rabbit hunter with two greyhounds walking up to the plaza and carrying dead rabbits by the ears. Louie reminded me about singing that cornball song in the choir and how we always cracked up when the green giant lyrics came along and "the valley was so thick with corn it would laugh and sing." Maybe I'll hear from him again. Dad never writes. Have to send everyone Christmas greetings.

12-14-65 Avenida de la Paz #16-2, Downtown Celebration

My five new friends who teach for Santiago Fuentes invited me on "Chateo." After classes, we five international teachers—French Maria Elena, Swiss Daniel Diserens, Portuguese Antonio Costal, Irish Timothy O'Hanrahan—went to five different downtown bars. At each bar, we would all swagger in to the smokey warmth, stand together, order *tintos* (red wine), raise our glasses, offer a toast to the wine or a curse on Santiago, drink up our *chatos*, talk, joke, nibble on snails, clams, cheese squares, anchovies, shrimp, olives–any kind of *cosas finas* or appetizers. After maybe 15 minutes and witty toasts like the one I learned on my birthday, one person would pay the five *pesetas* for everyone's wine, then we would all file out into the cold streets again and, laughing and calling and rioting, Antonio would lead us to the next bar where a different person would buy the next round for the group. (Martin Cane didn't join us but later told me the English for *chateo* is "pub crawl." News to me. I was the youngest and still learning to drink wine.) After five *chatos* and *cosas finas* in five different bars, we were feeling so jovial that even the icy wind pushing us toward our separate apartments seemed tolerable.

12-15-65 Avenida de la Paz #16-2, Quijotada

Took notes about teachers' exploitation last night at the cafe. Lots of financial grievances. Angered by finding out these issues, I wrote down everything they said. After teachers' meeting, volunteered to serve as their secretary. They agreed. My notes re Santiago's obvious exploiting: (1) refuses to allow teachers to offer paid classes outside his Am. Institute; (2) pays unequal wages to equally-qualified teachers; (3) charges for and expects teachers to do translations but pays nothing for them; (4) pays nothing for overload to teachers on monthly salaries; (5) pockets the entire 20% fee increase he charges for private tutoring off site; (6) underpays office boy, Luis, by three hundred pesetas a month. My new European friends are afraid to confront Fuentes. Not me. On the walk home, Antonio said *huelgas* were illegal in Franco's Spain, that I could be arrested for organizing a strike. Tim said the strike was *un quijotada*. "*Que es un quijotada?*" I asked. "As in *Don Quijote*," he said: "You ride in, attack an injustice, ride out again, go on to the next injustice." Have to read *Don Quijote*. Told them I was leaving Salamanca.

12-16-65 Avenida de la Paz #16-2, Strike Aftermath

This afternoon in Santiago Fuentes' office, all six of us stood and listened as the Portuguese Antonio Costal presented our grievances and solutions—orally and in my typed copy. Fuentes was taken completely by surprise. I watched his neck flush red with anger. His white shirt collar seemed to swell and, for a moment, his bow tie was going to choke him or burst. We allowed Senor Fuentes one day to reply, or all six of us would walk off the job on December 17. Friday afternoon, his words exploded from beneath his red mustache like Lady Finger firecrackers. First, he fired me. (Someone had squealed to Santiago that I'd been the organizer.) Then he fired Tim, the Irishman. Then he fired Daniel the Swiss. Then he fired Antonio the Portuguese. He gave the Briton Martin Cane and the French Maria Elena to the end of December to decide. When Santiago finished, we all walked out together—shocked, red-faced, laughing, satisfied. On Monday we learned that Santiago had increased Martin Cane's monthly salary by 1,000 pesetas. He'd also paid Maria Elena's back wages—unpaid since October—and increased the wages of Luis, the underpaid *botones*. And he announced that every professor at the Am. Institute would now be paid thirty pesetas per hour for any class. I could never go back to the Am. Institute.

12-19-65 Avenida de la Paz #16-2, Letter to Sister

Carol wrote, so I wrote back. Told her I hoped the tent was in the mail. Some days my fear of leaving the comfort of this room is overwhelming, other days my desire to leave this room is strong. She seemed worried about me, so I told her I was sure to return from this adventure with a rich knowledge of the Spain that has always been underneath the tons of history we don't hear much about. During the remainder of the winter, my plans are to see the people in places like Valencia and Malaga and Alicante—all filled with stories—then slowly move northward, migrating with the spring. I can live on about $25 a month which my Spanish friends tell me is ample cash. I'll live close to the Mediterranean where the temperatures are in the low seventies and eighties. Because I now have almost $270, I think I will have enough to fly home, unless something unforseen occurs. I told her that thinking about the unforeseen is to be caught in the whirlpool of a desire for security, so I don't entertain many of those unknowns. (I didn't tell her about my getting fired and getting drunk on my birthday because I know the folks will read every word I write.) I did reassure her that I'll return full of funny stories, tales, and without any money, and I'll be changed. So I encouraged her to keep studying and practicing—even if it's marbles in the dirt with some little boys outside the cathedral like I saw yesterday. As I write, I remember Dad putting up a string of flashing lights on the house that made it seem like a used car lot, and Mom painting a 6" stove pipe and elbow white, then making a huge candy cane by spiraling red crepe paper around it. I can see her now, studying the first present under the tree. The mystery of gifts, the reds, whites, greens, blues, will multiply, secrecy will increase, snow pile on the roof, icicles form on the eaves, and then music begins. I bought an orange from the street vendor for my non-existent Christmas stocking.

12-31-65 Avenida de la Paz #16-2, New Year's Eve, Salamanca

Time is as infinite as the sea, but there are only two hours left in 1965 for finite, living, breathing, believing, thinking human beings. In those last two hours of the most important years of my life, I will write down my celebration here with the Sanchez family. Festivities started at the post office when Feliz and I opened Mom's package—applesauce cake and fudge. I divided the cake between the two post office employees, Feliz, and myself. The Sanchez' beautiful oldest daughter came home from Madrid, brought Christmas carols no one had ever heard except me. We have just eaten a simple meal of soup, fried fish, and apple pie which is the main reason for eating the soup and fish. Apple pie may sound a little foreign in Spain, and it is but no longer, for this afternoon, surrounded by three interested housewives, I calmly kneaded flour and fat together, peeled apples, picked up the pottery dish with one hand, gave it a whirl and cut off the overhanging crust so deftly that might even have caused my Mom to blink. The pie baked perfectly in the gas oven, and as the fragrance filtered throughout the house, noses lifted with questions concerning "that smell." At midnight, we will each eat 12 grapes, welcoming in the new year with a grape eaten for each chime of the plaza clock. Some will go to midnight mass. It is the custom. American fudge will be passed around with Spanish hard candy. Later in the morning, we will go out for a walk with all the people singing in the streets, some drunk and others in a fit of happiness, and both will be indulging in their special form of extremism. Texas cowboy hats, whistles, confetti, Auld Lang Syne, flamenco, *cante hondo*, and bubbling joy: all is well beneath the cold stars in Castile. When those two hours are gone, we will have lived to feel how one year flows into another and time flows in shimmering streams of golden honey toward sunrise tomorrow.

6.
Salamanca to Lisbon
January
1966

VERTICAL FROM UPPER LEFT:
Headwaters from
 highway bridge
Eddie Bauer Tent
passport pages

CENTER:
Spanish calendar, '66

BOTTOM CENTER:
GV to EC aerogram

VERTICAL FROM UPPER RIGHT:
Portuguese family
 friendly driver
pocket calendar, '66

1-1-66 Avenida de la Paz #16-2, New Year's Day, Salamanca

Dear Mom, Dad, Dave, and Shorty—

Everything you have done, everything you sent, arrived Thursday morning. The tent and ground sheet are perfect. The plastic bags superb, pills welcome. I paid the customs fee of $11. Now, the rolled-up down bag sits on top of the pack, and just beneath it in a zippered pouch are my passport, new journal, etc. Inside the bag are two plastic bags of clothes; one for museum-cathedral occasions of dark green pants, dark green socks, white shirt, green tie, black shoes, and belt; the other for everyday attire like a change of underwear, sweatshirt, two pairs of white sox, tennis shoes, wool cap, long underwear, raincoat. Then there is a first aid kit of band-aids, Mercurochrome, chapstick, cotton balls, Halazone, and Dramamine, a sew kit of assorted buttons, safety pins and straight pins, Bondex patches, needles and threads. Also stashed away are a double plastic sack of therapeutic vitamin pills from Aunt Mildred, a plastic jar of protein pills, a plastic sack with tooth brush, tweezers, fingernail clippers, toothpaste, shoelaces, a plastic sack with a *History of Spain* and various maps and pamphlets on the country. The propane stove—a blue cylinder of about eight inch height and six inch diameter—and the threaded burner are stuffed right together. Then there is a canister containing rice and raisins to go with them, the leather pouch for my electric razor and a copy of *The Art of Loving*. On the outside in the three pouches which give the pack the appearance of a new *Katy-No-Pockets* or shoe bag, there are sardines, a large chocolate bar, 20 tea bags, a plastic bag full of powdered coffee, salt, sugar, and matches. The cook kit occupies one entire pouch along with an Old Spice deodorant container which houses my two jackknives, fish hooks, sinkers, leader, assorted trinkets for friendly gypsies, black shoe polish, and the remains of the shoe grease. The harmonica sings alone in my jacket pocket. The $230 in travelers checks are zipped into the collar of my coat, boots are on feet, new jeans on legs, plaid shirt on back, canteen and hunting knife on side, and umbrella in hand. Now if you want to come along, you'll have to walk because in addition to all that stuff, the tent fits in two slings on the front of the pack, acting there as a counter weight against the pack and sleeping bag. My straw hat from Ecuador perches at a rakish angle on newly cut hair, and let's hope it doesn't rain. (The olive oil for cooking is in a plastic bottle.)

My trunk is now packed and sits heavily in the corner where it will remain until I am more certain of my future needs and plans. The Sanchezes have agreed to store the Olivetti and the suitcases for me until that time, so I foresee no problems there. Dad, some of the stamp blocks were badly damaged in shipping, but I salvaged what remained to be sent home, along with brochures of the places (or at least some of them) which I will be seeing. So, when I write Malaga or Alicante, you will have some idea of the where instead of just the how, when, and where. I plan to do the same here that I did in Ecuador concerning your stamps: buy as many as possible right from the post office and send them directly to you. Hope that's alright. I suggest not sending any more letters until you hear from me again because once I have passed through Madrid and the embassy, I will probably not return north until spring. There is the equivalent of "General Delivery" service here called *"Lista de Correos."* Add the name of the city, and my name in Spanish: ***Jorge Venn***. If you put that on an envelope and send it to the city I will indicate soon, then communication will be restored. This is my last letter from Salamanca.

1-2-66 Avenida de la Paz #16-2, Leaving Salamanca

What drives me from this comfortable room and way of life to sleeping in a tent on hard ground? If I knew, then maybe I would understand why I'm in Spain and more about why I'm alive. The only reasons I can offer are simple and indefensible: I want to live a prodigal life, a transient life, a life of discovery that has no easy security except that which I supply, no future except that which I make, and no direction except that which I choose. A few months ago, conquering my fear would have driven me, because I now have no fear, I have grown. When I stood side by side with Jackie Almeida and we stared together at the sea from the deck of the *Cristoforo Colombo*, I was filled with longing to return again to the assurance of love in her arms. But she was gone. Fear drove me to this family, loneliness has kept me here. Now those fears don't come knocking at midnight dreams asking shelter for a wandering soul. I know Alice loves me more than I knew, but she is married and unreachable. I have found others in my state, others who roam the earth discovering the unexpected and asking for the unseen, for camaraderie, like Martin Cane, Timothy O'Hanrahan, Antonio Costal, Elena, Mercedes, Miriam, and the other students in the strike at the Institute. They were stalwart companions, that Englishman and Irishman, and to hear them speak one might think them to be arch-enemies. But they are men, as I am a man, and our company and conversations bore fruit and I always enjoyed their listening ears and company in quiet hours away from home.

But they are gone, Martin to Murcia and Tim to Galicia, and I am again left alone here beside the Tormes to watch the river flowing seaward. As the Tormes seeks union with the sea, so I seek union with humanity, with that great oneness that unites us all here on this planet in a common life struggle for existence. What is it that we have in common, and when that is answered, let us not speak longer of trivial differences, but of the strength which unity can bring yet always aware of the similar strength of disunity. That is what I intend to do as tomorrow I go forth with pack on back, pouch on side, heart in hands, searching for men who know what it is to feel the pain of love, the fear of death, the want of hunger, the gnaw of poverty, lure of the unknown. I have chosen this way of life to explore what unites men, what prevents us from continuous fratricide, what makes us like all rivers flowing toward the sea. Let us lay our yeoman soul bare of its trimmings, of its decoration and mechanisms for defense in society, and thereby encourage others to lay themselves bare in a similar way. For then and only then can we communicate as human beings in similar estates, then and only then can we understand what is essential and basic, what is at the core and not on the periphery of life. Martin, Tim, and I had begun to do that very thing, but time prevented us from further mutual discovery. It is time, that dirty stealing villain, that ruins all, that snatches life from us and takes away the fleeting aesthetic experience as fast as it brought it to us in some unsuspecting moment in the cathedral of forest or stone.

For tomorrow at this time I will not enjoy the comfort of this chair nor the warmth and joy of this family, nor the security of the foreseen day and its events, for I will be— where will I be? I don't know. I may be beside some cobblestone Roman road awaiting some driver of a modern chariot to befriend me with his horsepower, or I may be riding next to a friendly truck driver as we roll toward the Portuguese coast over a land too ancient for textbooks. Or I may be pitching my tent beneath the medieval walls of Ciudad Rodrigo, surrounded by children of inquiring minds, or by gypsies of acquiring habit. But wherever I am I have the naive confidence that my journey of discovery will be met with understanding, compassion, and a desire to see it succeed. Away with comfort, away with the warmth of brazier and family; I'll find them in new ways and new places—any place people keep their fires, build their homes, grow their gardens, anywhere in the din and glitter of cities too young to be historic and too old to be happy. So, good by Salamanca, bring on a new Spanish tomorrow. A few months ago, I could not have said that, but I say it, now, today: Adios!

1-3-66 Salamanca to Ciudad Rodrigo

Trucks brought Salamanca alive before the sun and, as street light shone through the Persian blinds, I knew the time had come. More noise from the street below, sizzling black tires in effluvia of recent rain, a watchman's hourly cry, starting engines grind, wind, roar. Then I am gone. Walking through misty light, I cross the Tormes toward Portugal. A truck passes, I make the sign, but the truck continues in the darkness without even the flash of brake lights. I can barely see the cathedral spires and the towers of Clercia shrouded in mist. Then, ahead, a hand beckons, flashes white in the semi-dark. I run, the pack bouncing, a truck driver asks where I'm going, then I stood in the rain alone. The signs said numbers and names but offered no words of comfort. Trucks and cars passed, their lights burning through thick fog of a cold Castile.

The man who stopped is a banker who usually wouldn't have stopped. A New Spain Spaniard, he told me—during the 90 kilometer ride—of his days as a student of Philosophy and Letters. Now, he said, he was serving the worst master, capital—selling smiles. I felt his frustration. "To write," he said, "the first person to meet is Hunger." An escape device, he called me, his SEAT 600 a confessional booth. Outside, the awakening country flashed by. Unknown men were forms against black earth.

When we arrived in Ciudad Rodrigo, I asked to be dropped by the cathedral, the least visited place in the city. After dropping my pack at the tourist hotel, I set off on a stroll around the medieval walls. Once grandeur and warriors, now men oppressed; once a fortress, now a relic, a museum of war. In places, bullets had pocked and shattered the cathedral and cloister walls.

Beside the river children—many children—came to watch me erect the yellow tent, then cook rice and steak on the propane stove. Who is this strange man from cowboy and Indian land? They played around my tent doorway and I felt close to them. Their innocence inspired no fear; curiosity was their deity. The sun set red and gold. Black cloud streaked the west sky. Evening stars rose cold. A man strolled by and said the last words of day as cathedral bells tolled nightfall.

1-4-65 Cuidad Rodrigo to Guarda

Stars at 7:00 welcomed another unknown day. The night was still around, hovering in the misty banks, in poplars that lined the Rio Agueda. In the city above me, the castle loomed all squares and corners, outlined by streetlight shadows. Breakfast was a hurried affair between me, the half-liter of milk from the canteen, a chunk of bread, chocolate, and the vitamin and protein pills. In the early darkness, women came down to the river to dip buckets of cold water. They asked me if I'd been cold. I replied honestly that sometimes yes and sometimes no. Because the yellow tent was soaked with dew, I set the stove inside and crawled out to watch the steaming prehistoric form there in the dawn. I looked up and wondered about the stars, looked toward the road to Portugal, and watched men walk past singing behind glowing cigarettes—pulsating lights that generate their friendly dots of fire without a passing whirr. Then I was gone walking along the highway, beside the route of men going toward Fuentes de Onoro or wherever the road might lead. The pack was heavy but my spirits were high with yesterday's success and my thoughts tried to penetrate the river mist that covered the faces of fields and men at work.

At noon, after many car and trucks had not befriended me, I stopped at a roadside park and fixed lunch. Rice and raisins, steak and onions, cheese and chocolate. The sun warmed my back and the tent drying on the fence. Cars passed, faces stared. I thought about them all in their hurry going places while I sat and watched, munching, chewing mouthfuls of rice and steak, sweet and sour. And I wondered if they all knew where they were going.

Then again the road. I had walked ten or twelve kilometers that morning and hope was beginning to fade when a car roared past. I made the sign and brake lights greeted my eyes. "Student?" "Yes." "Where?" Fuentes de Onoro, Guarda, Viseu, Oporto!" "Ha, ha, Good." And we were off to Guarda–city on the hill, the city that could not hide, the city towering, fearsome, an old Roman garrison town, an outpost of empire built on top of a huge mound in the landscape. The man, a business man, jolly, seeking youth and glory, rich, virile, balding 40s, but ready and willing to share bread and sardines and wine beside a stone bridge. A night's rest and now I am gone. "Everyone walks uphill in Guarda."

1-5-66 Guarda to Viseu, Portugal

Portuguese men do not understand Spanish. Walking downhill from Guarda, people going to market stared at the strange figure I struck against their provincial retinas. But I stared in return so we were equal. The rocks, rocks, rocks, walls put together like puzzles. A familiar white fir or hemlock greeted my eyes. The wind from Spain cut through skin and clothes to bones of passing farmers. Country people in huge coats with fur collars, one man tapping a calf gently, another swinging a lamb by its forelegs, another driving hairy pink pigs with ropes tied to their hind legs. Rounding a curve with the fat-faced farmer who had picked me up, we almost shot out into the endless airy heights of the Mandonga Valley. The river separates it almost symmetrically while on each side whitewashed houses with red tile roofs burnt brightly in a 9:00 sun. Olive trees flitted past, tires squealed against the cobblestone curves. Then he dropped me on the gravel shoulder.

On foot again, I shouldered my pack, a burden too light to be carried and too heavy to be left. Stopping in front of a signpost, I extracted the map from the pack to discover where I was. Knowing that I was somewhere between Guarda and Viseu made the orientation easier, and after asking a bread vendor, I finally realized that I was in Celerico de Beira where roads divide, where decisions must be made. Was it to be north to Aviero or south to Coimbra? North? South? South? North? Indecision killed the minutes as I stood by the road fork watching spring water flow from a pipe in the hillside. Behind me castle walls loomed in sun and shadow of early daylight. At the sight of a fortress, I imagine battles, swords, siege, shouts, agony, wounds, blood, death, treasure. Then, when a car passes, I watch the road again. Never can I stray far from its life-giving rides. "Yes sir, north to Viseu, from there to Oporto." Again, wheels roll, Portuguese mountains roll by, rocks and more rocks everywhere. It feels like an unfriendly land, but endless terraces grow grapes, oranges, wine, goats, sheep, olives. Here are men who know hunger, cold nights, hard days. In yellow afternoon sun, I see the river run cold, clear, run seaward, a river of spray, rainbows, mossy waterfalls. Populating the banks, I see women washing clothes on their knees, surging ahead and back, suds flowing against rocks burnished smooth with human hands.

My ride is a dealer in pesticides who watches for his competition, not his friends. His conversation was like chasing a squirrel or watching a soccer game. I was never sure which tree he was up or what subject had the ball. Any number of subjects led to others as we purred along toward Viseu."'What is the United States doing in Africa? Why should it care about Portuguese Africa? He fired off questions like 4th of July skyrockets that burn brilliantly and momentarily, then die into darkness. As we stopped in Viseu, I answered him: "You see those women on the sidewalk? If that car were to run up on the sidewalk and kill them, you would be outraged as would I. Not that our outrage would have any effect, but the important part is the expression of it. However distant the problem, the world is too small to ignore opposing ideologies and their propagators. We believe in our way of life and would like to see the Portuguese and Africans enjoy the possibility of similar freedoms. It may not be the best, but it has brought more people more happiness in less time than any other." With that I got out, shouldered my pack, and walked toward Aviero.

1-5-66 Viseu to Aldeana to Aviero, Portugal

Afternoon sunshine enlivened my cobblestones and spirit. On a park bench, I ate lunch, rested, then started to walk along the road again. Sometimes, I rested against orchard walls, studied green fields, orange trees, the ox team plowing on a far terrace. I wondered where fortune would lead from here. Down valley, up hill gathering more dejection as truck after truck passed without stopping, until I was determined to spend the night in my tent. But dejection lost again as brake lights flashed, tires squealed, a brown face emerged from the Opel. He looked almost Indian, but spoke to me in German. We were off again, my ride a hospital administrator who said he'd killed 100 Chinese one night in a front line Army post in India. Now, he was employed as a bricklayer in Germany, though he still came home to Portugal whenever he could. Conversation rolled as we rolled.

Suddenly, we drove off the main road toward village called Aldeana. It was the hometown of the bricklayer—rock walls, rock houses, rock-hard people, men of rocky fields. "We will take little lunch here," he said. I followed my driver into the shadowy maze of stone huts. Strong odors charged my nostrils at every step: pig sty, eucalyptus smoke, chicken coop, human sweat, baking bread, sardines. In one of the stone walls, we entered a small room and stood in semi-darkness. No electricity. No lanterns. As my eyes got used to the darkness, I could see an umbrella and a few chairs around the walls. Women without teeth and their dirty-faced children began to crowd at the door. For lunch, we stood around a wood table. My driver filled our glasses with light rose— homemade—and we drank without any bitter aftertaste. I didn't know how to eat the sardines, but the hot flat cornbread went down easily. Then, in a steaming dish with three forks, boiled pork fat and blood sausage appeared from the hands of a man but face of a woman, voice of a man but hair of a woman. The driver told me Aldeana was a very old village and very poor, rocks and vines holding them together. Before we left, someone gave him some huge turnips and a jug of wine. He threw everything into the trunk of the car and we drove back to the main road heading into a blood red sunset.

Curves, dangerous sharp curves, wove snakelike before us, and below us—down terraces of olive and cork trees—the Vogua River meandered to the sea. It seemed to do little to bless those who lined its banks. I swore the bastard driving was crazy until we arrived at his garage in Aveiro, and by then I was almost convinced. Hong

Kong had been his home for five years, Aveiro for ten, Viseu previously. Chunky with short hair, mustache outlining his incisive mouth, grim but friendly, soldier-sharp, militaristic, strong. As we ate dinner around his table in a large living/dining, room, I met his wife, children, dog, cat, and television. All evening, I was distracted by the rough whitewashed ceiling where beads of moisture condensed, hung, dripped. (I'd watched this in my tent at Cuidad Rodrigo, but had never seen such moisture indoors.) Sleeping was easy tonight.

After a breakfast of *anis*, *cafe con leche*, bread and delicious butter, my host drove me to Estareje where my thoughts had been for days.

1-6-66 Estareje to Oporto, Portugal

Estaraje, Rua Pr. Egas Munis, 321, was the destination today, to see Jacqueline the purpose. But she was gone, doors locked, and as my guide the postman told me, it was bad luck. Thank God the sun shone that morning, and that a 24-year-old housewife from the second story shone too. Her light was brown-eyed, seductive, inviting to coffee, cognac, chocolate, and oranges for the trip. Her damnation was the city and her "daddy" or husband, a 36-year-old lawyer who kept her at home as "a rooster his hen in the egg-laying hole." She was almost too nice when our hands touched, but after seeing her children and her house, the *niceness* changed to housewifely Portuguese hospitality, in spite of the fact she showed me her bedroom first. Helplessness almost overcame me as I stood there in front of that house where a woman I loved and dreamed of would have been home had I come a day earlier. In parting I kissed the housewife's hand and she waved three times as I trudged off dejected and hoping to make Oporto by nightfall.

Around lunch time, I'd waved and called out to three fishermen grilling fish over a fire: *"Que aproveche!"* I heard one say to the other, *"Un Espanol."* There was disgust in his voice. Then I understood I was in Portugal. My standard Spanish greeting and accent made me an outsider. My Spanish money was worthless. No place for American Express traveler's checks. Welcome to no bi-lingual no man's land.

Before a ride stopped that long afternoon, many drivers passed my extended thumb. When a truck driver, a mason, finally stopped, I climbed on the flat bed, and we were off for a wild ride over the coastal plain toward Oporto. The truck, a grey sort of monster called "Bedford," rolled along trying to commit suicide on the curves and fratricide on the straightaways. In back, I sat comfortably on the rolled tent, eyes squinting through slitted lashes at the countryside. It was dangerous to open wide because a fine sand-like dust whirled circles on the mason's flatbed. Now and then, one grain would slam into my eye as we rolled along and I would lose more than seconds of the scenery greenery extracting it from an inept pupil. Then roll from side to side, keep your balance, man, hang on, another curve. Where now? Is this the road? 90 kilometers an hour? He's turning off the engine? OK, to coast down the hill and save gas. OK. A freeway. The Americanization of Portugal? Here? Wait. This is 6 kilometers out of town. What? Get off here? Oh, hell. I jumped off the flatbed and my grey steed roared away. There is no mercy, but it's only 4:00 pm. A good sun, a good rest, and after a piece of chocolate and a shot of water, I can be on my way. About kilometer four, after no one had offered a ride and many had offered stares, obscenities, I was a bit mad. So, stopping by some ancient castle stairway that was mystically grown over, up and down with a Portuguese version of blackberry vines, I got out my silent harmonica. Now, music would be my stay, since man had gone his busy way. I made up songs, sang them, played them, and generally ignored the haughty freeway traffic. "Picking up cork on a Portuguese highway/ is not a bad way to spend your time/ if the cork on the Portuguese highway/ will help you along the line." Cork picker, stranger, right foot left,/ throw another thumb out/ right foot left. Who wants the cork from the Portuguese highway/ who wants the cork from along the way;/ neither the cork nor the man nor the highway/ had any use for it yesterday. Right foot, left foot, plug along man,/ cross the Duero in this foreign land./ Back muscles, leg ligaments why are you sore?/ Five more kilometers are easily in store." So I went, singing, halting, unrhymed, in shabby doggerel, and thereby passing the time over gravel that seemed infinite. Crossing the Duero I met two young sardine fishermen who were well-drunk, but well-met. They served as guides, although I could hardly understand, and we soon became conspicuous along the trollied streets where lighters and jack-knives' owners must have licenses for their possession.

I walked the 6 kilometers to Oporto and another 2 kilometers to the campground where I easily put up the tent, built a small campfire for meditation, sat by it for warmth, and remembered the Blitzen River and Mt. Rainier. Night dew, a rising moon, and sounds of street cries, trolley wheels and traffic roar lulled me into a deep sleep.

1-7-66 Oporto, Portugal

Light glowed through light canvas, casting an eerie glow over the blue nylon and green plastic. Outside on the front porch, dew had invaded beneath the plastic, while in the eucalyptus trees, heaving mists still suspended by formless branches hung like smoke beneath the tavern card table light in a Spirit Lake winter. Not wanting to do the tasks of daylight yet, I turned on my side in the warm envelope of feathers and silk, pulled the drawstring on "Many tried, None Equaled," closed my eyes again, and attempted to sleep. Outside, a man crunched across the gravel. About 9:00, I rose, cursed Portuguese timidity, rubbed aching tendons, and ate. Washing dishes was a concert of American pop tunes which the English lady in the "loo" overheard. We chatted briefly about my where and how but my why untouched. Full of suggestions on places, times, and seasons, they filled me full of good tourism. Then, after an abrupt dismissal, they crunched back across the gravel to their camper and I was again alone there, before my glowing stove.

I was tired, unwilling to see churches, castles, wineries, and slippery sardines, so I spent the remainder of the day doing necessities for my preservation. Lunch found me on a park bench beside cheese, sardines, bread, prunes, and Oporto boys for company. They had joined me after I began looking conspicuous beneath that huge monument and manicured shrubs. Talking, misunderstanding, eating, smoking, believing, wondering, questioning—all were part of the sardines shared there at midday.

I walked back to the Camping, bought milk in a bar, had a glass of Porto wine, and went to the tent. I had thought some about the safety of its contents while in the city, but decided not to spend my mind in worry. On opening the zippers, the decision was rewarded for all was untouched.

I spoke to the gatekeeper about his life. He was resigned to $11.00 per day and seeing his wife and children on weekends in a village. Wooden shoes clattered on the stones as we walked toward a cork tree. Slipping my knife from warm pocket, I handed it to the gatekeeper whose calloused hands took it and applied it to the tree. Once it was untouched, whole, and protected, but the life of cork trees is exploitation, skinning into nudity of bare trees. We stood there carving cork into a size appropriate for use in my canteen top. The cork tree in my canteen—shaped, sized, and fitting—is nothing like the fire in my brain. The fire I sat beside again that night burned into coals of eucalyptus, reflected from the rounding stones of fireplace, and as I crawled into my canvas cave to sleep, the smoke was still boiling away into the wind blowing through swaying trees toward the sea.

1-8-66 Oporto to Lisbon, Portugal

Rain tapping light fingers over the canvas awakened me to quick movements against the elements. Scrambling out into the first drops, I grabbed armloads and the pack, heading running stumbling toward the roofed bathroom, shower, kitchen complex. Returning for the tent, I jerked the stakes out of the sand, picked it up and ran again toward the shelter—dry cold, silent cold, white porcelain cold, marble cold, white lights cold. But in that cold was shelter, so there I stayed until the milk had boiled, bread been eaten, vitamin and protein pills taken, and pack arranged.

It was 5:00 am when I strode out of that gate toward the city, feeling desperate in the rain, feeling angry at the world, feeling weak in the calves. Determination rose to a splattering surface as I decided to walk out instead of take the trolley. "Walked into this place, and by God I'll walk out of it." Long strides, heavy shoes, relentless drops splattering dirty sidewalks, relentless eyes staring in the early misty light. Porto was busy early: bread vendors with huge baskets on their heads, fresh fish shining in the street lights, octopi slopping in pans, sardines like fingers of black silver shimmering. Then I became afraid, I lost confidence there in the oppressive rain. I wanted to escape from this ugly city—out, withdrawal, away, go, run, hide, race for the sun; south I fled without a backward glance, searching for warming rays of light that fall from friendly sky of white and blue.

Striding along the street, I asked people for the way, for guidance to escape. Few had the courage of ignorance, many the pointing finger of direction to the station; I sustained their misinformation, turned corners, walked down balconied streets to the smell of baking bread, across plazas, up hill, down hill, down hill up, right, left, where, there, and then I stepped out into a broad avenue of banks, sizzling tires, an excess of statuary. I sought the train station for escape from here, from this rain. "There, over there is front." Portuguese, contrary to popular legend, understood little Spanish.

The station was a huge cave filled with brown staring eyes or transients while outside, steam hissed from waiting metal monsters whose only life was already laid ahead in straight lines of steel ribbon. But mine was not that way, however badly I might have wished it straight with regular stops; mine was a growing rose spreading branches in all directions with little trellises, following instinct instead of some engineer's command from cold hands. Frustration mixed with the train as I tried to buy a ticket.

Not enough money of the right kind; but I bought it anyway. It was like wanting to move from the dormitory to Weeds my junior year, like leaving for school, like getting away to goodness. And I got away, fast.

While the *fulgonete* pounded out over the Duero river bridge, I sat staring out the streaked beaded watery window at passing tile, trees, children standing in dismal doors. The rhythm soon moved me to sleep a train sleep of fantasy without a pillow. Then, it was Coimbra, then Lisboa, and I had returned to the station of Scarface where those first waves of doubt had washed on a sandy brain in October. After two oranges for lunch, I walked down the waterfront sidewalk, looking at the finished Christ and the unfinished bridge that stood side by side on the Tagus. A voice in English asked if it could help, so I turned to meet a cross-eyed Californian just escaped from the Army in Germany. He was a hider behind words and cliches who never said much about himself or anything he thought. About all he could summon for conversational topics were his plans, his great personal accomplishments, and fatherly advice once he had discovered how old I was. To keep him going I asked questions, to get rid of him I made up stories, and to get away I walked fast toward the campground.

Afternoon 5:00 sun baked through the nylon and denim blues as I trudged along looking for a taxi driver who I thought might befriend me. His rotting teeth and bloodshot eyes I would not forget, and tried to pin them on every driver I saw fly by in a black Mercedes. He appeared, waved, and was gone. I cursed him, flagged another, and after driving my bargain, got in and rode to the campground.

1-9-66 Lisbon, Portugal

It was heaven, salvation, the Renaissance, Restoration, and Atomic Age all in one for the campground had hot showers, washing machines, and English-speaking people. I took a four-day rest, found a ride to Madrid, got renewed confidence, and found New Zealanders for company. I put up my tent and slept there on rocks of a covered patio. The lights burned all night, so sleeping was fitful—at best. Sleeping on rocks is like being a chicken on a spit: you must turn from one side to the other to keep from being flattened instead of burned. New questions: learning how to know when it is day; guessing where to begin once your sun has risen; deciding what to do in moments of linguistic void; how to not fall headlong into the gaps between Spanish and English?

1-10-66 Lisbon, Portugal

This afternoon I rode into town with the New Zealanders to stroll through Lisbon's portly streets. After walking past a thousand bars and little stores tucked away in shadows, I turned up La Libertad. There, fish swam in deepening pools, swans curled hose necks around, searching out that pestering flea, sparrows clicked in the bushes, pigeons waddled furtively toward breadcrumbs, while on the Avenue cars roared by in twos and threes toward fictitious destinations. I saw statues depicting men's struggles in war, straining over-muscled figures from Rubens and Van Dyck carved in stone for the glory of man and his country. Then some red socks jumped out as I passed a bench, Hawthorne and English entered to replace them, and soon the owner of the sox and I were talking with his friend, George, the first being Eric, over Portuguese coffee. They were half-brothers, world travelers, Alaskan fisherman, English teachers trying to be little Hemingways in Lisbon. George and I immediately fell into conversation about our mutual art and shared, in spite of his hesitancy, some ideas on writing. It was the first time I have ever had the opportunity to see another oriented toward creativity as I was and wanted to be. We drank some, spoke fervently, tried to be open, and found unconsciously a coming together unusual among men. As he so crudely said it: "It's as if you walked up to a girl and said 'Let's fuck.'" He quoted something from Keats about art that I liked and remembered—the difficulty of separating the dancer from the dance. So are we who put our souls on paper as inseparable from our art as its creator and performer? We disagreed, agreed, avoided intellectual calisthenics and becoming defensive, asked many questions, and exchanged brief histories, all the time moving deeper and more slowly into an understanding whose cause is shrouded in the mystery that is still the artist as a young man.

Eric happened to be swallowing mashed potatoes from the cross-eyed Californian intelligence officer I had met earlier that day. When a lull passed over, I dismissed myself to be alone, walking toward the campground and sleep. I could not think that either of those men could have anything to say to a society from which they are aliens.

1-11-66 Lisbon, Portugal

Tonight I wandered over to the trailer of a New Zealander who I had been told was a famous writer. Thinking I might learn from him, and also show him the *Prospectus* and "The Woodcutter," I knocked on his trailer door. His balding wrinkled face remained fixed on a magazine, so I knocked again. Still no answer. Then, looking more closely through the foggy window, I saw a hearing aid wire running down his chest. Winding up, I gave the door a series of short hammer blows to which he opened the door. I said, "Good evening, sir. I share your art and aspirations. Might I speak with you informally—as a friend?" "No, I think not tonight," he responded, "but thank you very much for calling. Perhaps some other time." Door slammed. I cursed him softly and walked away toward a soccer game under street lights. Why do men age into bitterness of vinegar, become hermits before the grave, and islands before continents? Protection? Remind me when I am old to always give audience to young men as equals, not sons.

7.
Lisbon to Valencia
January
1966

CENTER:
Spanish drivers on remote
bridge stop for lunch

UPPER RIGHT:
Crossing to Portugal

1-12-66 Lisbon, Portugal to Salamanca, Spain

Today, history passed like tons of wet sand as I rode with Elmer Malekoff, a chunky Canadian and his California wife and daughter. They were en route to Madrid then Rome, so I suggested we drive the route I had just traveled from Lisbon to Coimbra to Ciudad Rodrigo to Salamanca. A lawyer and engineer, he was doing UN research in Rome and he believed he had now cornered most of knowledge by degrees, lacking only the finishing cultural touches he was now putting on by a year in Europe. A friendly fellow but more likely a Faust hiding behind knowledge and words, he enjoyed high personal esteem and a desire to be quite right and authoritative. So as he drove, I played his game of sticks and stones, only trying to avoid offending my transportation to Madrid. Argumentation and dissent were his earmarks, qualification and the conditional tense his punctuation. But he gave me this long ride and befriended me, so I befriended him in return. Because he had no contact with anyone along the road, I tried to fill in some of the critical gaps that he often fell into as an over-anxious knight into a moat. And I was better informed than usual—which surprised both of us.

When I knocked on the Sanchez' door at Avenida de la Paz #16-2, they welcomed me again and granted my request to stay overnight in my old room. After recounting my travels and fortunes, I had a deep sleep. They said I had lost weight and changed color. That night, standing shirtless before the mirror, I noticed I was thinner, but that was no matter for someday I shall stop rolling and gather moss, drink from the same spring twice, and grow old in peace and memory of Spain and Spaniards, a curiosity satisfied, men seen in context. It would be hard leaving Salamanca, my friend Timothy the Irishman, and sandstone in a million forms.

1-13-66 Salamanca to Madrid

Out my window, I could see Malekoff's VW. Elmer, his wife and daughter were waiting below in the Avenida de la Paz while I readied myself for the day's travel. Leaving Salamanca, we passed curves and bumps, swaying and sliding across the *meseta* toward Avila, ancient cultural fossil with ancient stone walls preserved as in Spain in severe lines showing the veins of history. Malekoff and I finally came out in the open about our different perspectives. I proposed the thesis that one could not begin to understand Spain until he put aside critical eyes and began to see as a Spaniard saw the phenomena which make up Spain. Malekoff disagreed. His way of understanding all the strangeness which he saw around him was through comparing and contrasting what he saw as strange to what he already knew. From the beginning I had chosen to avoid such comparative thinking in an attempt to be a *tabula rasa*, thereby gaining some more intimate knowledge of how Spaniards lived and felt. In contrast, I wanted to divest myself of what I knew, or at least those attitudes which might prevent insight, but Malekoff wanted to retain all his old insights and compare them with new stimuli already understood. His approach seemed to limit discovery of anything new.

As we spooked through the Guadarrama tunnel toward Madrid, talking ceased as we each withdrew into ourselves to examine how much had been revealed in the conversation. For me, it was good, this learning how I thought, but for Malekoff, I did not know. For his wife, who had also found herself becoming interested, it must have been a time of recovery. They both seemed turtle-like, both in their ways, their personal interaction, in their conversation with me and their little girl. They had hidden their heads and hearts beneath an ethnocentric shell and didn't experience what a child feels, of knowing the newness of day, the fascination of hands, the intrigue of sounds, the call of smells, the joys and sorrows of coming and going. But then, I suppose they feel pity for me so I beg them to befriend me in my struggle, and in that begging, in that search for pity, they find themselves coming out of their shells by my agency. For I try—in my face, in my voice, in my words—to move them to compassion, to empathize, and thereby escape the dangers of stagnation, of emotional congealing, because it seems they are seldom moved to pity, or love, or hate, or fear, or anything that might be called an emotional response.

After parking in the exhaust-heavy air of Madrid and consulting the professional tourist office, Malekoff drove me to a campground west of town where I was prepared to stay that night. As we entered the gate, I cranked down the window to test the air. Cold. Our headlights soon hit those of a house of a grey-haired gruff old man and his wife who, feeling pity, asked me to stay in their house where the cold would be less. So there, after being shown to a cold cubicle with bed and night stand, I made dinner on my camp stove, then slept in a room whose darkness became heavier than wet sand. Phobia and imagination took over as I lay there in the dark, but fatigue soon conquered both.

1-14-66 Madrid Campground

I got up before sunrise to speak to my host. Walking together over the campground, I found him to be rugged, resigned, retired, but still ready for a new day's challenges. Children married and working in Madrid, he and his wife squatted on this land that once grew potatoes and corn. He now cared for tourists in summer. Last year, a German girl had come in winter—as I had last night. He invited her to stay in his home and she had lived with the caretaker and his wife for eight days and never wrote the letter she'd promised when she returned to Germany. His wrinkled face looking out over that cold morning in Castile, a cigarette smouldering in his mouth, he remembered that she had not written. Few letters would be as important. As we stood there watching fog shift and lift, the old man moved sand nervously with one shoe, and smoked and spoke thoughtfully. Listening was like watching a bird fly toward its nest in a leafless tree.

Then Malekoff came—his pudgy face and blue eyes slightly red and small. I shook hands with the caretaker, said several adioses, then got in with Malekoff and his family and rolled out the campground driveway. The caretaker had not charged me the 15 pesetas which he could have. I will see him again. Back in Madrid, Malekoff parked the VW on the street, and leaving his wife with instructions not to stray far from the car, we went hunting for habitations, cheap ones, in Calle San Marcos. Up dark worn wooden stairs to push a button, wait, footsteps, and the excitement of an opening door. After an hour and a half of searching, we finally found a room in a *pension* at No. 43 Calle San Marcos. On the third floor, filled with stale air, smelling like fresh wet plaster, at least the room would be dry and warm. Then we returned to the car to find his wife crying because she had been left alone. Malekoff said that was the way women were, and especially because of her period, she was that way.

1-16-66 Madrid Prado

Sunday afternoon. The Prado was open and free, so I shaved and changed into my good clothes and went there to see the paintings on *Anon's* suggestion more than anything else. *Anonymous* was a big influence because she thought of me as a writer and she wanted to be a poet—a mutual obsession. We influenced each other. Leaving Denver after a night together of layover, she had said something about love. She'd taken me to the Telemachus play, dinner, and had seduced me—first time—but I knew I just felt a kindness toward her. We wrote long enough to confirm that she wasn't pregnant. She was just not my type. Her beauty wasn't what I desired. Still, she was very smart. I admired her quiet grace. That was why I went to the Prado—she said I should appreciate it for her. I came out speechless, breathing deeply, and almost incoherent. For I could say nothing about all I had seen. All I could do was stand in front of those huge canvasses and stare, absorb, commune but not with words. Just stand there and let what is inside you feel what is there in front of you. Don't speak about it to anyone. Just look and let the truth and beauty penetrate and warm your soul, fill it with wonder, and let your imagination run rampant over the walls. It was too much greatness at once or was I too small to absorb it all? A lifetime to know, a world to see well. And would you believe I saw Lorne Green from TV's *Bonanza* walking the crosswalk ahead of me. Big head of white hair! From a distance, he looked tinted.

1-17-66 Madrid to Cuenca

After living and riding a week with the Malekoff family, I woke and packed my gear, my snail's shell. Before Madrid rustled awake, Malekoff drove me out to the highway to Valencia. On parting, I shook his solid hand, met his blue eyes with brown, and we promised to meet again. I did not envy his familial attachments, only his ability to channel energies into one canal. Perhaps he did that out of necessity rather than desire, but I did not know. Beside the highway, I stood in the early light–alone again on the sandy shoulder—and faced southward with hope. Munching fresh bread, chocolate, swigging the liter of milk, I walked with new power and rested muscles along the highway. Young boys and ragged housing project children came and stood by the fence wire, staring and giggling among themselves as I passed plodding along with my latest innovation—a hand-lettered sign meant to assist my travel: ***ESTUDIANTE, USA. ESPANOL- INGLES. HACIA VALENCIA.*** I made this for drivers who might fear my figure beside the road—gray pack, yellow straw hat, black umbrella, or for those who demand a planned, logical, rational world. I wanted to increase the possibilities by giving away my secrets–who, where, what.

Soon, a blue tiny van stopped—a pair of dogs in the back and hunters in front. I got in back for a 20 kilometer ride out of Madrid's ragged edges, riding with the dogs and breaking the law. The hunters were going out for whatever there was to be shot, not to feed themselves or anyone, just to go out and kill for a pastime.

When the highway divided, so did ours, and I dropped onto the sandy-gravel roadside. I had not remembered how cold and still feet can be, but soon discovered as I stood there, sign turning to those passing. The intersection offered many routes and kilometers and destinations, as drivers turned right and left, heading toward home or away. I started to think about Malekoff's befriending me but soon stopped because there was a car parked beside the road as if something were broken. I approached, asked their destination but was told that I would not possibly fit because there were too many coats and purses, pillows and blankets in the back seat. So, as they pulled away, I waved, turned, cursed softly at being left behind and looked up the road, away, around the curve that bent slowly from bridge abutments. There, after watching for another while, I saw a man dressed in brown and walking in my direction. As he approached, our eyes collided, strayed to the landscape, and then we stood face to face. He was tanned, yellow fingered from many cigarettes, almost my height and traveling lightly toward Malaga. After a few traditional exchanges, we both began to make the sign there beside the road. I felt close to this wayfarer, but he and I knew we could not stand there together and be picked up. For drivers don't fear picking up one *autostopista* but they do fear two. So again, it became a singular journey as he walked on ahead, hoping that whoever befriended me might also befriend him. As I write this my mind becomes very allegorical. I start to think about what it means not to be able to travel together in spite of common conditions.

Climbing out of allegory, I set my pack in the front seat of a Renault Dauphine, the same one that had said there were too many coats. So they had come back guilty? I chuckled to myself about the Spanish conscience condemning the driver on Monday. They said the farther they went, the worse they felt, so that state not being one easily sustained, they decided to return because of my cold feet. They were a mother, daughter, husband, son-in-law who just happened to be going to Cuenca. No, I didn't know where Cuenca was but some days back I'd decided to forgo my immediate destination—Valencia—and accept any ride. So, Cuenca, wherever that was, would be our destination about 2:30.

As we bounced along, I and mother-with-cold feet in the back and daughter-wife-husband son-in-law in front, she doing some map spreading and he driving cautiously, speaking at random, and winning all the arguments with mother and wife. They were bubbling with questions about the distant America, the near American, and the characteristics of both. I did my best to represent truthfully my self and country, wishing for more knowledge of both so as to better answer their questions. As we talked, rugged country passed outside in a dribbling rain. White-washed villages—dominated by the cathedral—became punctuation. Along the road, there were few places of pause or rest from the severe landscape. On the hills above us, there were crumbling fortresses mocking war.

1-17-66 Cuenca

A long afternoon in mist and history. The city was full of staring eyes, but I passed them, staring in return to change their stares into smiles. Few there were who experienced the change of face and fewer yet were those who replied to inquiring words. After leaving them, I found the railroad station, second and third class waiting room, secret, gloomy, smoke thick enough for cutting and packing hanging in the air like blue oil. Words and obscene pictures on four mortared walls added to an afternoon's passing, along with the man who came and went on hissing monsters from another world.

The Sunday watchman curiously came into the cavern, shut squeaking doors, and we talked through the smoke about him and his life, the war, his wife, bread, salary, and I loved the man for what he told me there in those moments when neither watch nor sun kept time. He lived in a railroad village nine miles away—one of those human settlements that sprouts beside the steel rails—and he'd lived there all his life. His family and wife stood as reason to live, work, and give, but there were times, he said, when he wanted to take the train away from there, as he had seen so many do, but he could not, knew he could not, but still that desire he nursed late at night as clicking boxcar wheels passed him on his watch. As we talked, more passengers came into the room, and not wanting to be overheard or just plain heard, he stopped and began smoking very intently, occasionally glancing up at those who came and went.

Most of the newly-entered passengers stared at me without words, so I spoke, opening the door for them. They poured in with questions, volunteered information, begat arguments among themselves, caught a bit of wonder and pity from me, and then they left, bound outward, away toward Madrid, Valencia, or wherever. And there I watched them climb the steps of train cars which carried them from this station to another. I fell into allegory again at their departure and began writing those hours in my mind for drama, someday, on a stage for men to see the power and reality of train stations and men passing through them.

Just before dusk, I stepped out of the station into the rain, opened my umbrella, and walked into Cuenca again to buy bread and to climb the streets to the old fortress. Houses hung, clung to cliffs, and the streets to their history. All were uphill. After glances over the fortress surface, I went back downhill to the streets where men passed on all sides instead of stones fixed up to separate tourists from their money. (It has always intrigued me how the Spaniards, after neglecting their history for such long periods, have now done almost a complete face-lifting, restored their battered fronts to make what was once unknown stone rubble into a proud past.)

I slid into a bakery where someone's grandmother was tending shop while her sister was away momentarily. We tried some conversation but I was too damned tired to carry the ball. The bread came, sister returned, I bought some sausage and left, returned to the train station, where a new group of passengers stared, silenced, as I entered the waiting room. Air was still, heavy. Smoke rings floated outward from rounding mouths, slowly lost shape but hung still, never falling, always moving, dropping caressed by sudden currents and then lost, engulfed forever by what once gave it form and substance. More rings dropped out, the people watched, brown eyes from black corners stared at the strange sight, and then I spoke to a knowing-looking fellow about Spain. He showed himself to be out of a mold, sort of refined aluminum but still in ingots on the dock. Perhaps some use if a furnace were near but otherwise very weighty. I told him what I knew of America in response to some general questions. That was all. Later, I spoke to the watchman again, then slept on the bench as trains came and went.

1-18-66 Cuenca to Teruel

All night I dozed a cat's sleep on the waiting room bench, my ears pricked in peaks, trying to listen and also to sleep. At 5:00 pm, I woke up to an empty room. Outside, a drizzling mist. Still dark on the streets. Trucks sat motionless. A dog's distant barking echoed through the streets. Occasionally a diesel would cough, choke, roar to life on a side street; otherwise, all was a humming quiet even the sound of sizzling tires. I wished for the sun and walked toward a gas station brightly lighted beside the street. A refuge, some company, a place out of the cold, directions, non-train station faces—those were my expectations when I twisted the cold steel knob and opened the door. "No," they didn't know if any trucks were bound for Valencia, but thought all had gone earlier. "No," I probably couldn't stay there and wait. God, how I wished for the sun. When I had my back turned, I almost cried for the sun, blamed those people who had brought me here, and sat on a barrel to wait. While there, I recanted the blaming, pulled out my harmonica and played, feeling the hot tea from breakfast bulbous in my gut. Suck and blow, in and out, up and down, the notes flew clear in the dawn. Men began to pass, forms humming on bicycles, walking in groups, alone, in pairs, heading for work before the sun. A bus trundled past, a few cars, more people, and the currents of humanity ran easily again. It felt good to have company on the streets. As I sat in the obscene light of the gas station, the company sign worked like an invisible magnet, drawing people down a common street toward a common destiny. My sign attracted some attention too, but by most was ignored. One truck driver stopped, said he was going to Teruel. I knew that was northbound and refused.

After another 4 hours of waiting, all the while watching the city's men trudge outward, another truck stopped and said he was going to Teruel. I threw the stuff in and was gone, away, to the northeast over roads too bad and country too severe to be pleasant. But the driver was a different story. From the lubricant south of Sevilla, he bubbled all the while with good humor, tiny laughs, and uncommon bigness of heart. Over the truck's roar, we exchanged jokes until the few I knew in Spanish were told. Then he continued the rest of the way as he butchered classical Castilian with an ease that threw me back to Ecuador. Subtle, dark-faced, flashing mirrors in the sun, teeth and eyes white to match, a ragged humorous real man driving with one glove off, shifting, wheeling the square monster around corners where rivers and rocks met dangerously, quietly close. Said he didn't like to race, was going to be a father when he got home, maybe earned about 1309 pesetas per day plus .75 cents per mile. His wife was again his life, but he said he still envied me standing beside the road watching and waiting for he might want to stop and spend a moment looking at mysteries with me. He was my brother.

1-19-66 Teruel to Valencia to Saler

It was 2:30 that afternoon when I jumped down from the running board in Teruel. I listened as Jesus gave directions for the truck stop café across the river. He said he was sorry to have to drop me there, but our roads diverged—his north to Zaragosa and mine south to Valencia—and he turned sadly, mounted the step, waved, and roared off in a shifting cloud of black diesel smoke. No sun in Teruel. Little mounds of snow lay freezing in gutters while roofs also had a white icing. I knew I could not sleep there. I walked to the truck stop Jesus had indicated. After waiting for drivers of trucks parked, drivers who did not come out, I cursed softly, went walking down muddy streets of a restored Spain 1940, past huge façades of stucco where children played in doorways. Then I stopped again, at the bottom of a slight hill, unrolled my sign to wait.

Many roars and blasts of exhaust later, a gray van pulled over slowly and I was away from Teruel en route to Valencia, long-sought land of cheap oranges, climate comfort, and city with history. My ride was a fatherly sort, a war veteran, and as we rolled across the hills outside Teruel, he spoke in bloody detail about battles fought and won along the road we traveled. There, he would say, 1,000,000 died and me, well, I was captured. Wrinkles in his face, greasy lids but penetrating eyes would then roll over the road and he would laugh as a soldier might on dying, a hideous sound, seeming to mock the thousands who once fought where we now rode in comfort.

The road and the man both wound upward into fog, misty haze too thick, like steam in a Roman bath. He became distant and almost began talking to himself. I watched, then tried to bring his wandering back by slender threads of questions about his family. As we began to drop onto the plain, he too came down in slow horseshoe curves of sentences, roads that never showed their future course, not even an insulting signpost to those the direction of a coming curve. He was the same way—unpredictable, soldierly, sly, still being carried on waves of war memories, evasive, hazy, inconclusive.

At Jerico, he said we were parting because there were no eggs to take into town. That's who he was, soldier turned egg man, retired with wounds as delicate as shells without gut. "War," he said, as I jumped down, "was not good but necessary." I answered not, because he was gone. Gravel and sand mixed like chocolate chips and cookie dough hit feet hard as I waited again. It was 4:30 in Jerico, and I knew an important hour was close. It was either ride or stop there that night. After several turned-down thumbs passed—a hay cart creaking like an old man, trucks roaring, men staring—I had given up looking expectantly at the road. Now, my eyes wandered inside the warm café, up on the cathedral tower, across whitewashed walls, into bursting straw barn. Where is the gasoline station? Is it like the church? Pump out the liquid and travel more miles.

Then, wham, the greyhound van with the old soldier in it came from my back. He said they had asked for eggs in Valencia. Now he would go home where wife, son, daughter waited for him only on weekends. A surprise visit, a good thing to do.

As darkness rolled in from the coast, I realized I would soon be hearing the Mediterranean plashing on Spanish beaches in little waves. Orange trees dripping with fruit lined the road on both sides. Old soldier told me how he had marched with Franco back along this same road when Valencia was taken. He pointed out where hundreds of Catholics had been loaded into trucks, unloaded, executed en masse by Russians during the war. Now, all that remained were names in streets carved where those believers had been killed.

I stuck my hand out to feel the warm air and grabbed some of the Moorish night, the Roman night, the Carthaginian night, the Cid's night. Then Sagunto flew into view as my soldier described the mass suicide by the Romans before the Carthaginians could take the town. Pavement, policeman, parks, questions, little boys for guides, kilometers, misinformation, no that bus doesn't run here any more, the Blue Line is what you want. Packs, weight, umbrella clicks along, men stare, while under my straw hat my brain says *keep going*. No answer from the body there on the right beside the road, munching, crunching, big chunks of bread. A bus following bright eyes came out of the dark. I waved. It stopped and we rattled on together toward Saler where I can stay at the campground beneath international pines. As I munched away on my sandwich, a little girl and her mother stared; they had a roaming curiosity too. I gave away my secret to them, butchered the verb *caber* to *cabo*—should have been *quepo*—giving the Valencianos on the bus a quiet laugh.

8.
Valencia to Alicante
January/February
1966

VERTICAL FROM UPPER LEFT:
Author at St. Barbara Castle by E. Cheney
cameo same site, 2/66

LOWER RIGHT:
E. Cheney at St. Barbara Castle by author, 2/66

1-20-66 Valencia, El Saler Campground

Off season. No one in the campground except Manolo, the caretaker. Good guy. Didn't charge me for camping. Set up tent under pines. Sound of surf. Warm gentle wind aired my sleeping bag on the tent frame. Tied a clothes line to pines, washed sheet, long underwear, handkerchief, socks, towel, and green pants—the ones with the permanent crease. Fine place to rest up. Manolo told me how to get the bus to the city. I'll go tomorrow. Borrowed his typewriter and desk, wrote a letter to Mayos. Told them my plan to travel south along the coast—Alicante, Murcia, Vera, Almeria—then come back here in time for Las Fallas on March 19. Manolo says big beautiful bonfires and fireworks, and girls dancing all night. Didn't tell Mayos about the girls. All the laundry dried and put away, goose down sleeping bag has loft again. Chocolate sandwich and tea for dinner. Played lonely harmonica a while, went to bed early.

1-23-66 Valencia & El Saler Paella

Sunday afternoon a lot of people gathering out by the café across the road and there were two men tending big wood-fired grills with big round pans maybe 16" x 2" deep. I could see steam rising and the surface bubbling, It looked like yellow rice simmering in both the pans. Something big was cooking. There were a lot of people setting out bottles and glasses and napkins and bread at two big round tables. From my place at the edge of the campground, I didn't know what was happening—it looked like a big picnic—but I wanted to go closer without being intrusive, so pretending to cross the street at the bus stop, I got a better look at the pans of what looked like rice. The cooks kept firing the smoky grills, and once in a while they added more liquid of some kind. When the round pans had stopped steaming, one of the cooks donned his insulated gloves, lifted the pan, carried it across the street, and put it down on one of the circular tables. That was a serious piece of lifting. People were gathering around that first table when the second cook brought the second pan to the other table, and then I was really surprised: everyone started dipping into the rice by using blue mussel half-shells like spoons. Then, some started to lift whole shrimp out of the rice with their fingers, and others took I don't know what—it was a Sunday feast. Both tables were surrounded with *Valencianos* devouring those huge pans of rice and sea food all cooked together, drinking wine, and toasting all around. I'd never seen anything like it. Made my mouth water, think of the 4th of July at home. Manolo told me the name—*paella*.

1-24-66 Valencia Walkabout

Warm day. Easy sea breeze. Took the bus into town. Left everything in my tent. Manolo is there. Says he's the "New Spaniard." Hours wandering around plazas and parks and shops and institutions. Walked by the Botanical Museum. Steel-barred gate was unlocked and open, nobody around. Benefit of off-season. Went in to look around–plants and cactus and trees and shrubs. Dead foliage. Looked like they needed watering. Down one path, I saw what looked like a grapefruit tree with big old grapefruit fallen all over. Looked good to eat, so I did a little foraging, stashed some in my stuff sack, walked out. Went to a park bench and cut one open. Looked delicious but not much flavor. Somebody's experiment, I guess. Oranges so much better. Cheap and sweet and easy to peel. Had a sardine sandwich for lunch. Wandered into one plaza where an old man with a cart and a small monkey were slowly rolling along and the man singing out "El A-fi-la-dor, El A-fi-la-dor." Had a round whetstone mounted on his cart. One woman came out, gave him two large cook knives to sharpen. Kids gathered around to tease the monkey and watch the sharpener pump the pedal that turned the stone. Monkey chattered at the kids, sat on the man's shoulder while he put new edges on the blades.

1-25-66 & 1-26-66 El Saler to Alicante

After breakfast, I saw this blue Ford Meteor 4-door—Canadian plates—stop on the shoulder of the highway. Topped with a 12′ aluminum fishing boat, the new car was towing a new 16′ travel trailer. Because of its size, the whole unit looked out of place, as though it needed an American freeway. Walking out to see this exotic machine, I could see the rear of the trailer tilted to the driver's side—a broken spring or shackle. A tall elderly man got out of the Ford. George Chennells and his wife Alice were retired from Alberta. Won a Spanish vacation. Spanish chuckholes. No Spanish. Needed a welder. They welcomed me, the bilingual kid. I talked with Manolo. Found a machinist close by. In the morning, they would drive to the shop, get the broken shackle welded, be on their way south. Manolo let them park in the campground that night. Got to know them—my second Canadians after Elmer Malekoff and company. Amiable, generous, ethnocentric, lost.

Wednesday morning, they invited me to join their North American breakfast—coffee, bacon, eggs, and toast—then we drove slowly to the welder's shop. He made short work. By that time, I was rested, cleaned up, packed my tent, ready. Told them I was going south, and asked if I might hitch a ride in the back seat. No problem. I told Manolo good by, said I'd be back for Las Fallas. Chennells drove to Alicante and we parked for lunch by the beach. Like riding with grandparents.

1-26-66 Alicante Beach

Watching Alice Chennells mix tuna for sandwiches in the parked trailer when a man's voice sang out a chunk of anthem "O Canada" and this middle-aged Anglo guy stood at the doorway and looked in. "Welcome to Alicante," he said. "You're a long way from Alberta." Turned out he was a Canadian writer, married a Spanish woman, lived here and wrote year around. We visited a while—named Doug Sanderson, pen name Martin Brett. Writes novels. Meeting two more Canadians and an Australian woman at a bar this evening, he invited me to join them. Accepted. I unloaded my gear. Chennells drove off to find a trailer park suggested by Sanderson. On a sandy flat spot next to an empty beach house, put up my tent, rolled out my bag. In front of me, the sea, the empty beach except for fishing boats pulled up above high tide. Behind me, the coastal highway, then terraced houses of Alicante climbed part way up the steep stone cliff to a mountain top castle. Almost nobody around. Across the highway, I noticed a bakery, a potable water pipe, a woman filling her jugs. Around 6, I found the bar and Sanderson with Al and Jim and the Australian woman. She wore a heavy blue pea coat—like a sailor. They were tourists, lived in a cheap *pension*. Been traveling together by train since France. Australian woman didn't like Yanks. Standoffish. Had a drink with them. Wondered if there was romance or sex at play. Before we split up, Sanderson invited all of us to his flat for a party on Saturday. Went back to my tent, met an elderly military guy walking the beach. He patrolled the coast all night against smugglers from Africa—*un guardacostas*—another new word.

1-27-66 & 1-28-66 Alicante Beach Camp

Chennells low on propane. Translated for them. Filled my bottle too. They took off for Gibraltar. Found the *mercado*. Bought a big round pan to cook for Al and Jim and Cheney—the Australian woman in the blue coat. Turns out she's an RN. We shopped at the *mercado* every day. They didn't know how to cook. Made fried egg sandwiches for everyone for breakfast, northwest beef stew for lunch, tea and something hot for dinner. Sometimes, I would help the local squid fishermen launch and haul up their boats. Once they gave me a calamari, showed me how to clean and cook it. Bit rubbery. Needs garlic. Al and Jim and Cheney have tight budgets, so they have to leave *pensions* pretty soon. Got to know Cheney better. She's hot, flushed cheeks, long black hair. One night, as I stood in the street below Cheney's open *pension* balcony, fierce sirocco started blowing onshore from Africa. Walked to the beach and found my tent flat collapsed with a big rock dropped on one side. Tent stakes in sand had not held. Pack full of eggs and groceries crushed by the rock. The *guardacostas* must have caught my tent blowing down the beach. Hell of a mess to clean up in the dark and wind and sand and spray. Got tent frame put back together and crawled inside, zipped up tight. Trembling canvas. My weight and the pack held it down. Surf lull. Not much sleep. Cleaned up egg mess in the morning. Thanked the *guardacostas*.

1-29-66 Alicante, Sanderson Party

Saturday night. Jim and Al and Cheney and I walked up the hill to Sanderson's flat—several stories above the beach. The large living room was crowded with Sanderson's friends—people dancing, smoking, drinking. He introduced his Spanish wife, welcomed us, showed the table of tapas on toothpicks, wines, beer, cognac. First social life in months. Felt awkward. Noticed Sanderson's typewriter and desk set up by the window. He was a real writer, I guess. Have to find one of his books when I get home. Night rolled along, Jim and Al and I watched the action and talked as more Alicante natives were getting drunk. One young guy got staggering and suddenly barfed and barfed right in the middle of the room. Shocked dancers stopped and stood back. Sanderson was aghast. He cursed at the kid. His wife would have to clean up, when Cheney stepped in, asked him to bring some towels. Without hesitating at the stench and smear, Cheney crouched down, started wiping up the vomited mess. Watching her, I realized she was admirable, fearless. I felt closer to her than ever before. I would never have done what she did tonight. When she finished cleaning up, the party did not pick up its celebratory momentum, and we all said our thanks and left. "That was a good thing you did," I told her. "It's nothing special," she said. "Nurses do it all the time."

```
2-5-66 Transcript of Conversation with Danti,
                    a guy at an Alicante gypsy bar
```

Shifting, averting, burning brown-black eyes, Danti said, "I'm ready to promote myself, or anyone who has something to say who wants to be promoted."

"What do you have to say?" I asked.

"Come over and I'll show you my work. I'm very serious about my poetry and music. I've studied music in this country for three years and will soon be publishing some of my work I hope."

"You writing in tune with the time, or something new?"

"No, it's really modern, like what is coming out now, but it's also me. But I get very tired of everything very quickly, become disinterested very fast in people, places, and things I do. I guess I'm a very restless sort of person. The only things I never tire of are my poetry and my music. I guess that's because they're all me and I don't tire of myself. If I did, I'd commit suicide."

"Where you from?"

"I was born in America."

"What part?"

"I was born in the south, raised in the Midwest, educated in the east. But I feel as if I was originally from France. Everything I think is a French thought. I have a thorough knowledge of French literature. All the great ideas can be traced to France, and since I intend to be great, it seems appropriate that I think with the great Frenchmen."

"You speak French?"

"Well, no, as a matter of fact, I don't. I started out to learn it several times, but dropped it. I'm funny that way, not sticking to anything, but I've begun again. I am to master it someday. That's one of my ambitions. The other is to become immortal, in one way or another, either by making myself immortal or helping someone else to become immortal."

"What's wrong? You afraid of mortality?"

"No. I just want to be immortal. And as a beginning of greatness I've studied the lives of all the great men. Men who have been somebody, rising out of oblivion, above the normal, to be someone, been known for who they were and what they did. Recognized, seen, admired, respected, my name on men's lips."

2-8-66 Alicante Birthday

Cheney turns 21 today. Jim and Al made a colorful card out of brown paper sacks. I made big apple pie, took it to the bakery across the street—same place we buy our morning bread. He baked it for me. Lots of laughs and jokes over Sanderson party fiasco. I played "Happy Birthday" on harmonica for her. She blushed at my singing. Sunset we sat around a small campfire on the beach. Got to know her a little more—bare feet. Great spirit, curiosity, seriousness, incurable romantic. Latest plans are to study obstetrics in South Africa, then travel up South America from Patagonia. Witty, pleasantly silly, somewhat proper, tendencies toward maternalism, tenaciously independent. As a nurse, she's confident of getting a job anywhere. Declined offers to be private nurse for wealthy oil sheiks at London Clinic. Too close to being a harem woman. Overwhelming love for horses. Admired the red fishing boats hauled up on the beach. Loves sunsets. Hesitant to sing. After dark, walked on the tiled *paseo* with her and Jim and Al to their *pensions*. Jim and Al are leaving tomorrow. Don't know if she'll go with them or not. There's a suppressed passion in her. Don't know if it's for me or one of them. She's taken everyone's photo.

2-10-66 Castle of Santa Barbara Lovers

Cheney chose me. After Jim and Al left, she moved out of the *pension*, moved into my one-person tent. Hearts high with kisses. We figured out how to fit both of us in one unzipped sleeping bag and it was a snug sweet fit. In the soft and suffused light of the city, we helped each other strip, felt the rising passion and whispered and kissed and I asked if she wanted me inside her and she said yes and we gently joined and fondled and caressed and rolled over and joined and moved together and her generous beautiful breasts touched my lips and my mouth and tongue accepted the invitations until she cried "No more, no more," and I withdrew before orgasm and we slept together there on the empty beach of Alicante, the tide coming in with our tide caught in the ebb of subsiding pleasure and passion. We didn't know what could be said now. I couldn't tell her about (anon) and my lost virginity. She didn't tell me she was *not* a virgin. "Why'd you withdraw?" she said. "Not time for babies now," I said. We lay awake to the sound of the surf, the gold moonlight shimmer across the Mediterranean. A perfect night.

2-12-66 Photos at the Fortress Reservoir

Morning-after dalliance, then hiked up the trail to the castle and Alicante water reservoir. Nobody around. Cheney took color pictures—jeans, sweat shirt, Ecuador straw hat. Posed for whatever she wanted: close-ups, by the fence, around the reservoir, on parapet, vista of entire city, beach, coast. Made some defiant smiles. She wanted to send pictures home. Read about the centuries of battles for this fortress, cringed at pouring boiling olive oil on attackers. Before we walked down, I asked her to pose in one of the stone parapets, and got a good image of her—happy in blue coat. After lunch, got out the map, started making plans for going south along the coast—who knows where. No suitcase but a good bamboo basket. Went to *mercado*, bought a length of rope, reworked the weak handles on her basket so she could carry her basic gear and maybe some food. (Had to abandon her suitcase in the *pension*.) We will leave in the morning. This beach will never be forgotten. Her long hair—deep brown with reddish highlights—falls easily to the tenth or 15th vertebra on her back, covers her breasts. Almost the same color as mine.

2-18-66 Vera to Almeria

Catching rides yesterday, the sky suddenly exploded, planes crashed, parachutes and debris came floating down. Black smoke billowing everywhere. Cheney was scared. Decided to leave Mercia and found refuge in an abandoned farmhouse just off the road to Vera. Put up the tent inside an ancient living room. Spooky but safe unless we got a direct hit. This morning, we got back on the road to Almeria, and everywhere US Army troops and vehicles are moving, like there's some kind of invasion. Still didn't know what happened until I got some news at a bar crowded with soldiers: US planes collided mid-air, lost 3 H-bombs at Palomares, a 4th bomb lost in the sea. Plutonium danger just 10 miles from us. Disassociated myself from the loud crowd of soldiers. Didn't tell anyone I was American. Have to get a Madrid paper.

2-20-66 Almeria to Benidorm Junction

Friday, we found a secluded cove away from everyone. Camped there two blissful nights—great swimming, vegetables with rice, blood oranges, read history to each other, sky a magical glow toward Gibraltar, darkness and starry quiet love. Looking above us, we could see the ancient Roman road Emperor Augustus Way. Cheney examines my body and comments quietly on the healthy color of my fingernails and I notice but don't share that she has deep strong arches and hammer toes from shoes being too short and narrow when growing up. Decided to start back to Valencia, so broke camp on Tuesday and walked along the highway going north. Green US Army trucks still crowd the way. No rides. Clouds of dust. Learn that they're trying to fish out one bomb with submarines, haul away the soil contaminated with plutonium. Place to get away from. Good rides got us back to Murcia around noon. Walked on the route lined with new apartment buildings with balconies overlooking the street. Some people called down their good wishes from the upper levels and two couples on the lower level invited us to get out of the sun a while, offered water and *sangria*. Goes right to my head. As we headed north, Cheney admired some whitewashed houses with red trim and planters, took some pictures. In another mile or two, I heard a street vendor calling "El Sillero, El Sillero"—and eventually we caught up with this little gray man singing and rolling an old wheelbarrow full of parts and tools, hoping someone needed a chair repaired. An ancient profession, this calling out your passing services, like the *Panadero* in Salamanca and the *Afilador* in Valencia. Lots of Sunday traffic to the beaches.

2-22-66 Benidorm Junction to Saler

Got a good ride through Alicante to turnoff to Benidorm. Waited there a while. A gray VW bug pulled over—it's Tuesday night, 3 masons driving home to Valencia after work. Little crowded to fit us in–I sit in back between two guys, Cheney is passenger in front with driver. Given the potential danger in this situation, I pretend to not speak or understand Spanish except simple commands. As we drive, I learn the boys have been drinking, then start talking about sex. The driver is, apparently, endowed with powers the others don't have. Their plan to rape Cheney becomes clear: get me drunk, two guys overpower me, driver has his way. At the campground at Saler, we dropped off our gear and set up our tent, the masons invited us to dinner at a restaurant in town where they bought us eel soup and bread and cognac after cognac—they were getting more drunk than Cheney and me. In English, I was trying unsuccessfully to alert her to the danger As they drove us back to the campground, the driver issued a new rule: "No more talking in English." Half drunk, the masons started singing "He's a jolly good fellow" in Spanish, so when they sang their last verse I told them I knew one more, then to the same tune they used, I sang "You've got to pass out at the camp ground, you've got to pass out at the camp ground, or everyone will rape." She glanced at me, and understood. So, when the VW pulled into the campground and stopped by the caretaker's quarters, she opened the door, got out, and collapsed her 160 pound 5'8" body on the ground. *Ay Dios mio*, the alarmed driver got out to see what had happened, fondled her breasts. The two guys holding onto me decided to let me get out too. I kept saying *Malo, malo*. Just then, Manolo, the friendly keeper of the campground I'd met weeks earlier, came out, saw me, and asked what was wrong. His appearance turned the rapists' plans to dust. We carried Cheney to the tent and rolled her inside, then they started to apologize. "Didn't think she had so much to drink," the driver said. "Very sorry. Very sorry!" All three masons got back in the VW and took off. Never saw them again!

9.
Saler to Orgaz
March/April
1966

VERTICAL FROM UPPER LEFT:
bomb clipping from
  Spokane Chronicle, 4/9/66
Fence Post Red Ball Capitals
Spanish Calendar, '66

VERTICAL FROM UPPER RIGHT:
pedestrians on tiled promenade
Alicante beach: tent, cliffs to St. Barbara,
anonymous swimmer

3-13-66 El Saler Campground, Valencia

Dear Mom, Dad, and Dave and Shorty;

Since the last time I sat at this very typewriter, I have been along more than one road, mostly in the south of Spain, and mostly in the city of Alicante. What I did in that city is, of course, now history. But its effects will be felt in your lives as in mine for the remainder of my life in North America or wherever it remains to be lived. Her name is Cheney, Elizabeth Cheney, Australian nurse working in London and in Spain for a sort of escapist vacation from the routine of walking and working between two doors. She escaped to the beach in Alicante and backed into me cooking fried egg sandwiches for breakfast, stew for lunch, and tea and something easy for dinner. When we collided, I turned around and rather unexpectedly found us reading history on a beach, exchanging short histories over extra tall glasses of hot milk (which she insists are quite healthy if you sleep on your right side at night), and discovering curiosity in word and action, laughter and seriousness, running and walking, that we had a mutual desire called permanence.

If you saw her apple shined cheeks and a presence of health might first jump out at you from the 5 foot 8, 160 (that last figure is secretive), long hair almost the color of mine falls easily to the tenth or 15th vertebra on her back, and her bare feet might complete a picture roughly drawn. Great spirit, curiosity, seriousness, incurable romanticism, adventurous (latest plans are to study obstetrics in South Africa and then travel up South America from Patagonia to Idaho), pleasantly silly, somewhat proper, tendencies toward maternalism, tenaciously independent yet ready to fly wherever migration lanes lead, easily engrossed in *The Source* by James Michener, a fine book for you Shorty and you too Dad—typist, shorthandist, knitter, tennis player, overwhelming love for horses and red fishing boats beside the sea where waves break, sunset watcher, camper, moralist of Christian caliber, likes Tchaikovsky, but hesitates to sing, ready for a trail through woods or exploration of some Moorish farmhouse, and capable learner, excellent nurse, something of a tomboy, quite ticklish, warm and yet reserved, a bit unaware of the listening world, and drastically patriotic: those and a few other phrases might begin to describe this woman who is seated beside me reading *The Source*, waiting until I finish this letter so she can read about herself, and read what I am sending to you and saying to you about her. Someday undoubtedly she will sit beside you Mom, or serve a tennis ball to you Shorty, or chase you up a trail Dave, or comment quietly on the healthy color of your fingernails Dad. A phantom of delight when first she gleamed upon my sight, a lovely apparition sent to be a moment's ornament. I have forgotten the poet, either Byron, Shelley or Wordsy, and to be a life's ornament, not a moment's. And on second thought, not an ornament for that calls up something decorative that is put away; that she is not. It also calls to mind something fragile and seasonal; that she is not. For what she is becomes real as you watch, chat, poke, and concentrate on her. You will hear more later.

After staying in Alicante for almost a month, I whirled on southward to the town of Murcia, old, completely Moorish and isolated from tourism, it provided an interesting porthole from whence you might see the infidel as he was until expelled in 1492 by the holy Christians; those from the north who got a Papal license and called on God at the same time. From there I went from Moors to Americans in a little town called Vera where we had the misfortune of losing an atomic bomb in the sea. Now the American Navy is offshore, the sea is cordoned off and from the distance which we viewed it looked very unreal. From there a couple Canadian fellows and I thumbed on south to Almeria, where gypsies live in caves, fishermen dry their crying nets and the wind whistles down over the Via Augusta, built by the Romans and still used and standing, a monument to their achievement, a mockery to the modern camp ground.

(*Handwritten from here on*) I have now left Valencia, have spent four days in Madrid, and am now in Toledo en route to Seville where I will be for Holy Week Festival and the Spring Fair. Healthy, browned, somewhat thinner, wiser, enchanted, and drowning in history, I will hope tomorrow to arrive in Cordova (?), spending some time there and then, on April 18, sailing from Vigo for London where I plan to study, work, and wait for the long-in-coming summer. Write to Sevilla, Lista de Correos. Will be there until April 12th.

Love and apologies,
(signed) George

3-15-66 to 3-19-66 Fallas, Valencia

Amazing is all I can say: Cheney and I go to the city every day, wander among the sculptures being finished, have ear drums pounded by fireworks louder than I've ever heard. Made the ground shake. People everywhere, people from all over the world. Cheney wasn't enthralled after we went to an exhibition in a plaza where buildings had been loaded with strings of bombas above our heads and the explosions seemed to never end. You could see the fiery fuse burning from bomba to bomba. At the end, everyone clapped. Had sardine sandwiches for lunch. Cheney doesn't like fish—afraid of bones—so she had a sausage instead. Met Cheney's friend Lex Van walking around with an entourage of girls. He's Dutch, footloose, fancy free. Good guy. Knew him from brief visit in Alicante. Traveling, living on the economy. Knew more than we did about the parades and sculptures and fires and bands and traditional costumes, but not much. He strolled around with us a while. Cheney had a visit with him. Out of her hearing, he asked me my intentions regarding Cheney. Haven't talked with her about it. Get married I guess I said. She took his picture with the girls. During the day, we watched the men build their weird fantasy sculptures. Fascinating—creating something which you will destroy. Wood scraps, carpentry, paint, cardboard—I don't think I could do it. They had judges and a deadline for competition and last night all of their hard work was burned down. What magnificent irony—destroy what you create. You have to love fire, spectacle, drama, transformation. I didn't get the satire of the sculptures. Fireworks were best at night. You could hear the bombas from far away. Got back to the tent late every night, but not too late for love. Manolo gave us some oranges, apologized for the masons again.

3-20-66 to 3-25-66 Valencia to Madrid

Left Valencia, lots of traffic heading north after Fallas. Got a good ride about half way to Madrid where we would separate—Cheney going to Paris then back to work in London and me going to Toledo, Cordoba, and Sevilla for Holy Week. We found a room for the night at roadside inn somewhere around Tarancon. Cheney traveling lighter now, we didn't have much food on hand, so asked the landlady if she had anything to sell. Fresh lamb chops a pair. After we finished eating—asparagus, potatoes, and chops—I asked Cheney, "Why'd you tell Lex to ask me about our future? Why'd you say nothing to me yourself?" She looked at me very strangely for a few minutes, didn't reply, walked over to the bed. Again, her silence surprised me. In our three weeks together, our talk had always been open and non-judgmental, so I asked again. Now, she turned her back on me, curled up on the bed, said nothing. I began to wonder. "Have I done something wrong?" I asked her. Still no reply. "You want to tell me something?" I asked. Silence and more silence. "I'm going for a short walk. You want to come with me?" No answer. So I put on my jacket and went out, watched the cars pass and the stars come out. Through a window could see the landlady frying her own chops now. Standing out there alone in the half-dark, I waited fifteen-twenty minutes, guessing that Cheney had somehow been offended by my question, so I walked in and went over to the far side of the bed, looked at her face to face and said that I was sorry for asking her about Lex. She was sobbing softly now, so I lay beside her and put my arm over her and tried to comfort her. "It's nothing," she said. "It's just nothing." "Can I make you some tea?" I asked. "That would be good," she said. We both got up from the bed, and I boiled the pot for tea. Thursday morning, the 24th, we got a good ride to Madrid and checked into a room in Calle San Marcos, the place I had stayed before. Her train to Paris left the morning of the 25th. Before we said goodbye, I promised to come to London to visit, and she gave me the unused mileage on her URAIL pass, forever changing my travel style. She had written to her family and I had written to mine. I told them we were thinking "permanence."

We were lovers now, and there was this new and inexplicable silence between us.

3-26-66 to 3-29-66 Madrid to Aranjuez to Toledo

Walked to Aranjuez, the pouring whitewater of the Duero everywhere, leading me to remember Cheney again—love of woman, the newness of her body, her closeness and warmth, her voice and touch have an indelible and unforgettable effect. Her nature is protective, comforting, and all-inclusive embrace. What human being is there who does not at one time in his life, desire the virtues of woman? Is there man or woman who shrinks from a protective force? I am tired, indecisive, worried, and yet find my life today, March 29, filled to its riverbanks with love for a woman distant, a woman near, a woman receptive.

Today, I arose to shouting voices of the youth of Toledo, those of last night who quickly sought my company in the sunset on Tagus outside the city's walls, the ancient city, mounted on a hill, a fortress unconquerable, a capital of three worlds, a refuge for three cultures.

Spanish past called that morning for investigation on the hill, but being almost drowned already in history, I jumped into the Spanish present to catching carp barehanded in a muddy pool left by the high water. The strategy was effective, and when the first sputtering, stuttering, grime-faced kid drew his hand out of that mud-hole, a cheer went up. *Que carpa!* And Juan, Julian, and Jose were fishing with uncommon vigor. I thought it might be the bullfighter in them that animated their fishing by hand, but they were concerned about my eating. Pants rolled to knees, river rolling in muddy foam behind us, a poplar grove sprouted in the moist sand, each tree being a resting place for floating flood-riding debris. Three hours and 20 carp later we marched triumphantly back to camp, then up to the fountain where cleaning, scaling, and decapitating took only a few quick flicks of the knife.

Our fish, however, were flavorless so I had oranges, bread, and chocolate for lunch instead of carp. Swimming and stories, bragging and knocking each other flat, and throwing rocks across the river—all this and thoughts of Cheney filled the afternoon until sunset. Clouds changing sun and spectrum colors, wine and sardines, finished the day with Toledo boys. I detected their admiration but did not acknowledge it.

Leaving my tent tonight, I mounted the thousand steps to the city by some ancient unused gate. One girl called me a 'rat,' her companion, a 'gypsy,' and when I flashed a flurry of swearwords, reddened ears ran home in the dark. I sat in one bar, studied the map, settled a bullfighter argument, then hunger moved me away to another bar where I devoured a sandwich and absorbed a newspaper. Men in the background cursed the church and loose women while the bartender wiped, smiled professionally, and wished the clock slowly ahead. I wrote 50 words, then dropped down the stairs lit by a crescent moon and a star-sprinkled sky. I thought about the men who had seen those same formations in an unchanging sky, about Ben Ezra and his friends, and longed to read Browning's poem again. Strange birds called, shadows crawled. The river slid noiselessly toward Portugal. There were no gypsies haunting my riverbank.

The Alcazar is not real, but Guardia Civil defended it for three months, grinding wheat for bread with a motor bike, making grenades from cupped door nails. Russian bombs flattened it, French cannons demolished it, yet it will stand another destruction. Once-rounded towers now jut squarely at four corners, stones sit where bricks once rested, stables now crumble where a new military government will stand. They told me a cadet from the military school swam the river, climbed the statue nude and hid the bronze sword before the police came. Cameras clicked, police came, smashed cameras, redressed the cadet and marched off. Where a general's son died because of his father's command, a plaque rusted away surrounded by creeping ivy.

Toledo, a high city, naturally defended by river and walls, where man can walk on popes and kings, see Jewish synagogues and Moorish mosques both turned Catholic now, wander through vein-like streets seeking the atmosphere of past greatness only to find modern Spaniards facelifting their history and enslaved by the same. To be Moorish is to be mysteriously delicate, decorative, finesse and detail, gracefully smooth, curvaceous in quarter tones of brown and green.

3-31-66 Toledo to Orgaz

A cloudy afternoon in a quiet valley. One Guardia Civil patrolled the roadside south of Orgaz. He was a bulldog sort—gruff, thick-necked, ready to do his duty with his shiny black tricorn hat.

"*Su documento de identidad, por favor,*" he demanded.

"*Qual, mi jefe?*" I asked him which document he wanted.

"*El unico que tiene, porque tiene un padre, una madre, un pais.*"

"*Pues, es al fondo de mi mochila and seria much trabajo a sacarlo.*"

"*Si no lo saca, no tengo recurso mas que llevarse a la carcel.*"

So, I unzipped my pack, unpacked my clothes and kitchen, fished my passport out of the bottom of my pack, and handed the blue-green document to him. He took it from me, studied it a minute or two, then said:

"*Este documento no tiene valor.*" This document is no good. It was issued in 1943. It is very old and no good. You must come with me to the jail."

"My chief," I said respectfully, "it's that you don't read English. That says "birth date" not "date of issue." He handed the passport back to me. I thanked him, packed up, and started walking south again.

10.
Orgaz to Seville
April
1966

UPPER LEFT:
Cadiz flamenco clapping

TOP CENTER:
close-up of GV's rucksack

UPPER RIGHT:
Toledo boys after
fishing for carp

BOTTOM CENTER:
Valencia for Las Fallas; *left to right:* GV, five unknown women, Lex Van (pointing at E. Cheney)

4-1-66 Orgaz to Cuidad Real to Manzanares

A driver stopped. Got in with a 35-year-old man from Cuidad Real whose major depression was that his 5-month-old daughter had just been operated on. He proved to be bigger than his tragedy, and as we talked and rode, he proved to be probably the most memorable Spaniard I have met. A graduate of Madrid University in Mining, his life previously had revolved around football and bullfights, but now those put aside, he concentrated on work. Why did he pick me up? "One must be human," he said.

Train from Cuidad Real to Manzanares was quiet except for the conversation with an olive grower who had left the farm to become a mason in Valencia but wanted to return to the farm. Sipping milk from a corked bottle, he complained of a bad stomach and slept. That night I pitched my tent behind a gas station on the main road south. Rain overnight. In the morning, a woman attendant asked me if I got wet. (First train ride with Cheney's pass. Suddenly everything is easier.)

Simile: as (dangerous, shaky, unsure, improbable) as two birds mating on a telephone wire. No one will get their message.

4-2-66 Manzanares to Santa Marta Mudela

As I write before sunrise, there's the grinding of cartwheels in the streets. Voices talked all night beneath my shuttered window. All yesterday, walked in rain and wind from Valdepenas to St. Marta de Mudela. Few drivers passed. No one stopped. I almost lost faith. Cold rain poured. No pity for the soggy form in the rain. Not asking for pity. Just some slight indication that we are all human beings—today, I was wet and walking, you're dry and driving. Tomorrow, we might trade places. For the first time in Spain, I appealed without success to common humanity. No stories. Got acquainted with La Mancha rain pounding the umbrella. Grateful for the waterproof blue jacket. About dark, I walked into Santa Marta, rented an upstairs room, took off all my sodden clothes, shivering hands huddled over my stove, made tea and sandwich, steaming clothes and gear laid out everywhere. Glad Cheney wasn't on that road. She had no protection. Should have checked the weather. Almost dry.

4-4-66 Valdepenas to Cordoba

The train to Cordoba sang no song today: a woman nursing, men cursing, the long sidetrack wait, a tunnel, black, an unlighted experience.

Off the train and wandering the city I came to two old Moors working quietly in the *Diputation* at 3:00 in the afternoon. Both a little over 4 feet tall, topped with black berets, faces spattered with whitewash. When I entered, one came down from his ladder, the other ceased nursing a bucket, and both began to give me a guided tour of the municipal government buildings as if they were their own. If craft and care imply ownership, they were owners. First, they showed me a place or the seventh stair where a Civil War bomb fell. Next a series of cracks in the veined patio glass caused by American sonic booms. Then, upstairs into the government assembly hall where portraits of preceding rulers hung in proud poses. Both wounded in the war, these old veterans both chuckled as they told me of a picture that had once hung in the assembly chamber—a picture of a father seated in thought, on his right hand an overturned bread basket, on his left brown-eyed, hungry children asking for bread. One pointed to the empty space above the door. The picture had been taken down and stored in the basement because of the Communistic overtones of poverty before the war–when men had no bread. Earning 60 to 70 pesetas a day, they were both fathers of six and seven children and still had no bread, but still prepared and smelled the banquets for officials and counts and still cleaned up after them. Notes of pride sounded as they showed me walls they had made. Strains of age sounded as they told of the war. Strains of sadness accompanied their admission of age and position. I asked where the toilet was, read a few of the dirty jokes on its walls, then left after a firm handshake and gracias with each veteran. I felt they were wise; left them singing, glad to have contacted real Spaniards again.

Statement: You put on dark glasses to protect your eyes and now you cannot see.
Simile: as tame as park bench pigeons, yet as elusive, for they flutter out of reach of
    even the innocent little boy who only intends to feed them.
Metaphor: pigeon's neck personality that swells and struts around females.
Inscription: in Cordoba's Plaza Mayor:
    I would rather die taking two steps forward
    than live a hundred years taking one backward.

George Venn | *Walking Spain: A Young Writer's Journal (1965-66)*

Persona: Truth becomes a dark brown face, smooth, among the shadows of a Moorish garden where orange blossoms whiten in spring, where a figure flits fluidly from path to path at dusk.

Simile: as a man who sees the world with only one eye, without depth, levels, or context

Simile: as boring as a bass drummer in a ten-mile parade.

Meeting people here who call themselves world-travelers and brag of adventures, miles, and wines, but have never known a Spaniard. If they did, it was only three fingers of a waiter's right hand on a glass of wine. These are tourists who, unconcerned and unaware, pass through this place beyond the touch and voice and sweat and tears of human beings. They are the traveling specimens who speak English to a Portuguese, German to a Chinese, then raise their voices and wonder why these people have not learned English or German. If people are to survive, they can no longer be of one culture or one time, ignorant of history, language, culture, and macrocosm. If such people are uninformed, they can be as conspicuous and undesirable as the Catholic church implanted in the middle of the Great Mosque in Cordoba. Both appear uncomfortable to the point of sacrilege, especially when we know the results of hate bred through ignorance, fear through isolation, and crusading idealism without compassion.

Table Talk:

"You are almost Andaluz!" Jose Poka said to me. He's a rebel against libraries and door to door existence, Hungarian who shared pastries and beer, aspires to be a writer. A great man, a new traveler, but more the student than the tramp.

A German said, "If it looks like a better place up there, give a wave." He forgot to say what to do if there was no place better. "You do my exploring for me," he said.

Another German said, "French men are distant and cold."

Half an hour later, I was eating shrimp, drinking white wine, and eating bread with three French history teachers. Our common tongue was Spanish. "This is the way we avoid war," one said. "A peon bullfighter was an ordinary human being, but was made extraordinary by his followers."

"If they hand you your passport, that is good, but this afternoon an official stood there by the door and threw my passport to the desk. He missed. I had to pick it up. This man will not take that. He tells them to take the street. That's so you remember Cordoba."

4-8-66 Cordoba to Seville

The road was full that morning. Five other hitchhikers had already gone when we were all picked up by an errant 22- or 23-year-old who lived by driving German cars to and from the Spanish car market. We arrived in Seville and I escaped the crowd as soon as possible, found a good secluded place to pitch my tent again. Began my wandering. Processions abounding. So much to see, crowds everywhere. One day I took to the Moorish heritage, the next to the Jewish, the next to the Christian. The Moorish heritage drew me most. For centuries, their lives resolved in tiled intricacy and design—no human figures allowed. Unending, mysterious, arching, suspended, deceptive, infinite: all the while to be appreciated while patterns are imposed on its superficial disorganization. At home more with clay than with stone, more in shaded garden than boiling sun, Moorish art remains to be understood by those who now walk in its shadows in the Juderia. There, narrow labyrinthine streets lead into white-washed dead ends, patios, painted potted flowers, poly-colored tiles and courtyards that still enjoy the shade of the green and bitter and enduring orange trees.

Surprised to see Lorne Green on the street: star of *Bonanza* in green-brown slacks, hush puppy shoes, white hair, dark glasses. Met a legionnaire of the Spanish Foreign Legion. Stationed in Morocco. Taught me his call for help: *"Ah mi la Legion."* Anyone can join, no questions asked. Eventually, I tired of Seville's morality plays, allegories, icons, candlelight, incense, drums, tears, wild flamenco, hoods. Oh how the blessed 2-ton Virgin came trembling along at midnight on the shoulders of many men. (How do we live without so many blessed icons? What is the Anglo equivalent?) To escape from ghosts, mysteries, and people of the city, a place I could spend a lifetime exploring, I chose my own mysteries, retrieved Cheney's aerograms from Correos and used more of her generous rail pass tickets to mount the all-night train to Madrid. Riding north in the dark, I read her blue aerograms by dimmed lights and copied some passages here to always remember:

> "My Mum said that she thought she got the message of your letter and asked me not to fall in love and get married—said it would be a stupid thing to do and not like me, but that is too late for I already love you and it is very like me. I hope you have a ball in Seville and enjoy holy week.

If you want anything, just let me know. I am having great fun here but I miss you to bits.

* * *

It sure is nice to see Loretta again but I was surprised to find that you seem twice as close to me and more important than my six years' solid friendship with Loretta. I was also surprised at how close she is to a nervous breakdown, as she has confided in me..."

4-9-66 Seville to Madrid

Riding free on Cheney's rail pass again, I rolled into Madrid station at 9:00 pm on the third-class mail train—the same track on which she left and where I saw her last. Felt lost love's presence there, her last smile, last wave. Walking around in the dark and rain looking for a pension, I found none. Hungry, soaked, tired, wanting the warmth of Cheney and clean sheets, I paid to sleep alone in a strange bed. In the morning, I sat down to write letters in a hotel of a thousand brown-marble tables where Cheney and I once sat together. Dishes rattled and silent Spaniards smoked and stared. Madrid traffic rushed by. I had *café con leche y pan*, wrote Cheney my plans, then wrote an expurgated version to my parents: lived on $90 for the last three months, had $140 left for London.

    A poor, white-haired woman sits between two doors in the hotel of a thousand marble-topped tables. Sad-faced, she waits with sagging eyes for men and women to pass in and out of the toilets. Her only hope for survival lies in the key she holds tightly between wrinkled hands, and in the roll of paper in her torn apron pocket. If you enter looking urgently at the locked door, she asks: "You want to use the service?" Half-smiling, a third embarrassed, you nod as she moves, eyes lighting up slightly, toward the locked door. There, she inserts her key and deftly flips the lock. Then turning, she looks up and says: "Served, Sir!" You ask if there is paper. She again smiles happily, reaches in the torn pocket, and tears off the normal amount. She waits. Do you pay her? Is she salaried? Her hesitation answers. Dropping silvery coins into her hand, you both move on—relieved.

New Noun: a *pylon* is a tower of power for high voltage wires.
Conundrum: The bull asks the bullfighter, Am I fighting your cape or you?
Metaphor: for the truth seeker life becomes an irresistible movement toward lights
    which shine through a forest at night.

11.
Madrid to Southhampton
April
1966

VERTICAL FROM TOP:
Torero & *capote Las Ventas*
Santiago Martin, "El Viti," bullring, Madrid, from Spanish Calendar, '66

S. M. "EL VITI"

4-11-66 Madrid to Avila

On the northbound train that Monday, I was sitting by myself next to the window when a middle-aged woman came into my car and sat down several seats back and across the aisle next to the window on the other side. When she sat down, I glanced at her but she avoided eye contact and kept looking out the window, her grey-black hair tightly wrapped in a dark scarf. Many Spanish women appeared to be severe, as though they might have lost their husbands or sons or fathers in the war and were now in mourning for their lives. But from my experience on the road, I knew that this was usually a defense against any advances, a strange mask to keep themselves protected. I turned back to my window and looked out at the other trains pulling into the Madrid station, the long lines of shining steel tracks and black crossties under the huge quonset roof, the smell of diesel and creosote in the air, the quick hissing of steam and the drip of water somewhere all around. The train suddenly lurched, each car behind the engine jerking with a hard whack of steel on steel, as the engine took the slack out of the couplings that protruded like fists between the cars. Gradually, the lurching arrived at our car and the train began to roll toward Avila and Salamanca. I glanced over at the woman once more and caught her looking at me—my Ecuadorean straw hat still on my head—or at least, looking in my direction. I pushed back my straw hat and smiled at her, but she looked away again: out the window there was something in the Madrid's endless rows of rectangular brick apartment houses that fascinated her.

After the train had passed out of the city and into the country, I got up and checked my packsack and sleeping bag and tent to be sure they were all still secure where I'd placed them, then walked back to the point at which the cars joined. When I sat down again, I said hello to her and we started a conversation: Elena Santero was a widowed school teacher returning home to Avila after a weekend in Madrid, and she asked about my story, so I told her towns and cities. By the time we reached Avila, we'd become friends—at least more than acquaintances, less than lovers. Memories of Cheney and sex. When she invited me to stay with her that night I wondered what would happen. Her dinner of pasta and sausage was wonderful, her bed was huge and warm and empty. As I lay awake alone in the dark in a strange bed, Eros seemed to disappear, though I fell asleep wondering if she wanted me. First sleep in sheets in months. After pan and café con leche and manchego and fruit, she gave me a tour of her famous walled city, made us a three-course lunch, then I thanked my hostess so kind to strangers, boarded the train to Salamanca—again using Cheney's pass.

4-13-66, Avila to Avenida de la Paz #16-2, Salamanca

Arrived in Salamanca about dinner time and found the Sanchez family in mourning for their father who had died of a blood clot just 15 days earlier. Sr. Fulgencio Sanchez was only 64. A short, surprise illness of only four days. That heaviness of heart was still with Teodora and Feliz and Luisa, and each one gave me a cause of death, but all agreed that he died while sleeping. The last I saw him in December, his vigor, ignorance, bull-headedness and Spanish temper were all ready to rise red-faced to the surface. My only regret for him is that he never saw the sea. Otherwise, his life seemed to pass without excessive pain, some adventure, many simple pleasures: family, smoking, wine, birthday and saint's day celebrations, short journeys through Castile, enjoying the worship of son and daughters as a puppet tyrant, having a bagful of sayings, a headful of off- and on-colored stories which he told with a special theatrical manner, and a pocketful of small coins. Not often did he sing glad song or sad song, for his was a song of complaint plus criticism. Unable to supply remedies, but ever ready to condemn, he jumped feet first into every discussion and often left the same way. Fiery, sometimes a shouter, a doting grandfather, malleable husband who had his outbursts, he was always ready to be silenced by his wife or self whenever the tirades became absurd. He died without realizing his desire to become an actor, his wife beside him asleep. And now over a dim lamp, dressed in black and dark rosary, she prays for his soul. Everyone is shrouded in seriousness while he may be laughing.

The Sanchez' granted my request to stay overnight, so I packed my two huge suitcases and typewriter stored for me, and I left on the train in the morning—last Cheney tickets.

4-13-66 Avila to Avenida de la Paz #16-2, Salamanca *(cont.)*

To salute and remember Fulgencio Sanchez, I wrote down some of his oral traditions:

"Los civiles son facil militarizar, pero los militares son dificiles a civilizar."
(Civilians are easy to militarize but the military are difficult to civilize.)

First Speaker *"Ha oido usted del cura pobre?"*
Second Speaker: "No."
First Speaker: "I haven't either because there aren't any."

"Hemos comido como obispos." (We have eaten like bishops.)

First Speaker: *"Me cago en la leche de su puta madre."*
(I shit in the milk of your whore mother.)
Second Speaker: *"Y yo en la tuya, por si ocaso."* (And I in yours, just in case...)
(Worst vulgarity possible and reply—only the First Speaker was offered by FS)

"Ojos que no ven–   (Eyes that do not see.
Corazon qu no siente."   Heart that does not feel.)

First Speaker: *"Que hay?"* (What's available?)
Second Speaker: *"Mucho y mal repartido."*
(Plenty, and its badly distributed)

"A la liebre ida, palos en la cama." (Rabbit gone means sticks in the bed.)

"Limpia, fija, y da esplendor." ("Clean, stable, and splendid.")
(Royal Academy criteria for admitting new words to Spanish.)

"Si no sabes cantar, no cantes. Si sabes canter, canta, pero en la calle."
"If you don't know how to sing, don't sing. If you know how to sing, then sing, but in the street." (Bar sign to stop gypsy singers?)

———————————————

"A mal tiempo, buena cara." (In hard times, a good face.)

———————————————

"Por los reyes, lo conocen los bueyes." ("The donkeys know the kings.")
(Proverb for 6th of January, Dia de los Reyes)

4-14-66 Salamanca to Vigo Journal

Using the last of Cheney's EURAIL pass, I rode the all-night train through Zamora and Orense. Arrived in Vigo about 9:00. Off-season free at the empty campground, I placed my ground sheet on a concrete slab, pitched my tent just a short walk from the fishing village. I could always hear the pounding Atlantic surf just over the big dune. Weather reminded of Santa Marta. Rained for four days in succession. Tent shed the water but with no fly still got wet. Got a bunch of old news papers from the bar for sleeping bag insulation. Every day, I tried to dry out, made breakfast, then walked up to the bar, sat down, ordered a cider, bread, and *queso de teta*, talked with the natives. As with all the other places, I learned about the cultural distinctions of this region—dialect, kilts, highland dances, hard cider, *queso de teta*—a Celtic heritage. To dry out and get warm, I sat in the bar. If afternoon weather broke I watched the seagulls hovering around the fish wharf drain, awaiting, sliding on invisible currents, employing an untapped wisdom of flight in the wind. Another day I walked down the beach, found an old fortress and slogan still inscribed, decided to try that in a poem.

The Fortress at Vigo

Walls of blackening granite acquiesce behind emerald
mosses, behind Tennyson's flower.
History loiters here smoking its silent pipe.

Stronghold where men died for kings,
here history changed chauffeurs. The bastion
still commands the lowly from high ground.

Watchdog of harbor and sea, fortress
fists overlook Vigo's eternal *sardineros*
mending their nets of silver.

Here rage once joined cannon roar
to gain uncivil ends. Now white-haired
hobbling silence rests on rubble piles.

Rusting bricks, crumbling mortar lie
exiled from usefulness, while shattered
granite become mute witness of war

On one wall of empty windows this epilogue:
> *The value of infantry is founded*
> *in the fighting ability of the RACE.*

No other reminders of battle. Only sea and river
winds play invisible games through the bones
while on the beach below *sardineros* ask:

"Do you know our war?"

———

First time to write like this!

4-14-66 Vigo to London, Letter Home

Dear Mom, Dad, Dave, Shorty, and Doug:

Greetings from the million bricks and rounding bowlers city known for centuries by the Thames looking up at Big Ben, Westminster Abbey, Tower Bridge, and cloudy restless sky with pigeons soaring high over Hyde Park where anyone, on Sunday, can and will attempt to convert the listening ear.

To arrive in this ancient city, I sailed from rainy Vigo on the Atlantic Spanish coast on the 18th on board the *M.T. Monseratt*, a converted California-made freighter now the best passenger liner on the Spanish Line. Companions, both Spanish and English, made the trip more than just a voyage over swelling sea: met a young Spaniard leaving home for the first time, feeling the pain of separation and knowing that his destination would not speak his language; met Matthew Port, 19 or 20 year old talkative English university student, a serious frilly-haired chap who graduated from Eaton (spelled without the a). Prone to convincing men of their erring thoughts and ready to admit his own; gave him my only copy of *Prospectus*, my literary editor debut. Met a blue-eyed Irish Jew named Jacob who said he knew the world's great people. When I asked him what maturity was, he replied "Maturity is liberation, my son, liberation from the plagues of pride, wealth-striving, to know the hierarchy of values, the government of forces, and essentials, yet be above them all." He seemed enigmatic, mysterious, wise. On deck in the afternoon between Spain and England, he called himself a failure at 65, then went back to the bar. No seasickness. Had Dramamine left from the Atlantic crossing back in October.

Some difficulty in entering England because of a shortage of funds and patience with the immigration officials. After rather an FBI sort of harassment, they finally gave me permission to stay for 30 days only. To remedy that, I have sent a check to the bank in Spokane requesting a negotiable check in London for $160.00. If it comes and if the immigration officials will accept that quantity as sufficient funds for living until June, then I will stay in London and England, waiting for new and plans from Aunt Bubs company. If it is not accepted by the authorities, then I shall probably find illegal work until June.

I cannot remember my position on the map when I last wrote, but I think it was

Madrid. From Madrid I took the train to Avila (Ah-vee-luh), unexpectedly staying there overnight with school matron with whom I made friends on the train. After a night of sleep in a bed for a change, breakfast off of a table, and lunch in three courses, I left for a difficult stop in Salamanca. After an all-night ride on the train through Zamora and Orense, I arrived in Vigo about 9:00 am. There, it rained for four days in succession, stayed in a campground for nothing, and the 18th, sailed away from Spain with 11 pesetas in pocket, two huge suitcases in hands, pack on back, tent on side, and expectation all around at the thought of England in April, seeing Elizabeth again, and just the newness of the place.

Having not received a letter for some time (having not written one either) I hardly know what to comment upon there at home. Will someone please bring me up to date on the world of Spokane, Washington?

Enclosed is an income tax form I have filled out which lacks only the figures off the W-2 form from Joe and Betty that should have been sent by now. If you Dad would send it to the proper address, I certainly would appreciate it. There is no duty or penalty for filing late if one is abroad, but proof of being abroad must be submitted according to the regulations I read in the American Embassy in Madrid. For that reason am enclosing my University library entrance card from Salamanca. Hope that will suffice.

Am seriously considering returning in time to work in the harvest, but that is still undecided. By the way Dave, a belated happy birthday, and to you too, Dad. Writing every day now and am trying to get something published here in London.

Write when you can.

12.
London to Spokane
April/May/June/July
1966

VERTICAL FROM UPPER LEFT:
Icelandic girl with bananas
Spanish calendar, '66
Eddie Bauer tent assembled 1/1/1966

VERTICAL FROM UPPER RIGHT:
Olivetti portable
Icelandic Air plane
City Literary registration, London, UK 6/6/1966

4-20-66 British Visa and Immigration Office at High Holborn

Walk on those black and white tile squares. Will they let you stay?
Sounds of counterfeit wind sings a duet with murmuring voices in a back office. In front are seven glass booths, some empty, some with voices giving permission behind black counters, plastic, smeared, fingerprinted and shiny dirt. In front of the blackness of counters, white fog of glass, plaster white of shirts and pink faces of men waiting.

Sweating gray like a mule skin; benches that feel like flypaper on fire.

Men smoking silently, impatiently, tapping feet, sweating hands again.

Papers rustle, men stare at infinite dots among a ceiling white, counterfeit sky of diffused light that never clouds.

Beside me, women speak Italian, in front are Indians. Spaniards laugh in corners; men with carbon skins and crimson tongues sit properly. Children chase rolling coins across tile floors, at ease, entertained, unaware of wary adult eyes.

Old, restless women in non-woman voices call out numbers as they walk through in green nurse uniforms, gold lettered technicians on typewriters and cigarettes with mahogany smelling fingernails. "Please wait until your number is called."

Slowness, order, calm impose themselves in the room. Be patient, accept it all.

Tolerate inefficiency if you want to stay; take what they give for another day.

Some hold hands, others sleeves, other men rest elbows on knees, some cross legs and uncross, some fold arms. Black men think they wait longest, white men wonder why they wait. Jaws grate on gums, ghosts in green pad through again, go out behind slammed doors gold-knobbed. Every thing lives on little numbered cards held up, noses indicate condescension. There are no friends, only dignity put on like face powder, importance like a backless jacket on a man without hindsight. Machinery for men and of men clanks onward, noisy gears ungreased, bearings without balls.

Spaniards laugh louder in the corner. Atmosphere pales to white to grey, soothing, brown, therapeutic, anemic. Some eyes flash anger, others indifference; others endorse the boredom, excuses float like rubbish on a river, disgust, insult, humor, amusement, wonder, amazement, gamble, tolerance, safe, reliable, courteous, sacrifice.

Telephones do more than men…take it, like it, smile and break…you must, if you want to stay because givers of permission are parrots of authority. Anything for permission. Give us your endorsement by buzzer or stamps. No smiles, only stares. "Where is number 100?" Scribble in notebooks, numbers go higher, footsteps drive nails across black and white squares. Pale ghosts move through air and sound without movement. Some wrap up minds in newsprint, then stare at floors, frustration, illegitimate foreign bastards away from mother. Little, brittle gold voices mock heaven, asking names in silver-black, dates, places, authorities, spellings, eyes pouring distrust over documents and faces, ask more proof, disbelief drowns confidence in faithlessness.

Jamaican, West Indians, colonialists: carry your passport proudly, son: Frenchmen squirm on sore bones, Germans ask belligerent questions. Then restlessness, disquiet, expressing a discontent to neighbors who never disobey. Telephones ring unanswered. Nothing happens. Silence. Monsters' footsteps of padding feet. Listen for the wind? It is air-conditioned without direction. Sighs. Parents preach patience, people make pilgrimages to bilingual toilets, relieving boredom, pressure's nephew in the night. Waiting, waiting to be given permission to stay. Look for the sun? It is 90 watts on switches without heat. Numbers grind back and forth along rusty pipelines. Marching from glass boxes as to valleys of death, commanders, machine-ice cold, like black telephone box plastic in winter.

Then questions finally come like vivisection by patriotic scalpel, questions come after numbers, personal, probing questions, professional smilers paste on their product to white teeth. Stare ahead, men, watch the white gods work who say you can stay in the world, watch the puppets, spigots of authority disperse their waterdrops of importance. Listen to wham, bam, whukp, umpph as rubber stamps hit the page. "Come back tomorrow please." Distrust colors the air, demanding acquiescence, a bowing down form replacing spines' curvature with minds.

4-25-66 Lucie-Smith

One Friday evening, Cheney at work, I left our sixth-floor love nest and walked to The Poetry Society several blocks away at 21 Earls Court Square. Seated on the second floor of a hot high-ceiling room with chairs in rows, I listened to Edward Lucie-Smith, a chubby, dark-haired man with soft skin and hands, feminine lips and smooth words, read his poems. First time I'd heard anyone read their own work aloud. A stimulating audience of dilettantes, snobs, diligent, Negroes, Italians, Scots, and many other new and unknown people made up the seven o'clock crowd. Afterward, some tried to nail me down by my accent and wouldn't let me up. Good group! I had tea and cookies for sixpence in the basement where Lucie-Smith always looked at the floor. There was dandruff all over his dark blue coat fastened with one strained button over his belly, and when I looked for his eyes, all I saw was oiled hair and thick glasses.

4-25-66 to 5-27-66 Southhampton to Earl's Court, London

Beside me a red rose floats in a clean, unlabeled peanut butter jar; on the floor Cheney's eight-month-old kitten bats at papers and scampers after shadows; above me one lightbulb shines; in front is a sink; to the left of that two beds and between them a television; then the door and chest of drawers; then a closet, fireplace, kitchen stove, and cupboards. Everything is quiet except the kitten which Cheney bought yesterday, and my traveling Olivetti. Outside, lights and nights of London simmer on, cars start and stop, a cold wind blows up the Thames, but none of that touches the kitten or the typewriter because we are inside where only our noises compliment each other.

Cheney found us this sixth-floor flat at Courtfield Gardens just off Earl's Court. She works at St. Matthews hospital nights, sleeps as Spirit Lakers used to sleep, leaving me free and alone—hours to wander and write. Worked on a short story. Our passionate energy, our hush and squeaking bed frame made us hot lovers wish for privacy and surf and tent on the beach at Alicante again.

Since arrival we have made several short trips together on days off. I have done my share of museum and gallery visiting, and often I take walks along the serpentine in Hyde Park. The city and its ways contribute little to solve the human problem of impersonality: a fear of one's fellows discourages conversation, a lack of relaxing hours prevents neighborly chats. Each man pursues his rising or falling star, almost unaware of the galaxy in which he lives. London is a huge city but the kitten is very small. The typewriter has no size at all.

Oh these billion bricks and rounding bowlers, the Thames, Big Ben, Westminster Abbey, Tower Bridge. Cloudy sky with pigeons soaring over Hyde Park Corner where anyone on Sunday speaks freely on anything. I delighted in the magic of sheepdog trials. At the museum I found my anti-specialization image: the heir birds became extinct because they could not feed without the male to chisel a hole with a short bill, female to extract the grub with a long curved bill. Right on!

On another London Sunday wander, I met the "Cockney Sparrow" outside the Tower of London. This man lay bound in twenty-two feet of steel chain, wrapped inside a grey sack, locked with two padlocks, and endangered by two swords shoved through the chain. Whips cracked as men bared to the waist performed for charity feats of escape in the cold afternoon wind. Questioning a small boy near me, I learned that these same men had been doing this same act when his father was a boy. He calmly explained the entire process of escape, boy-like in hesitance, until the invitation came to close in on the bound figure. Then, because the boy had no money, he left.

Image: Pigeons throw off a fine white unimportant bit of feather. Sparrows gather them for nests in the lilac. Usefulness is a feather blowing.

5-20-66 London Night, Earl's Court

A bewitching, metamorphic Cinderella hour is 11:00 at night in England. Then, the thousands who have nursed, cuddled, seduced, or just drunk from the many-faceted mugs in a foggy pub, emerge from their caves in pairs usually, or looking for pairs, as they, by law, must now go home. Some stagger out, others run, still others have left before 11, and of course, there are the stragglers who want to cherish the last drops or just have the rare privilege of being the last to leave. Then, on the sidewalk of unfriendly cement, their late laughter after 11 bounces off into side streets and Mews, their swagger-stagger-sway of bodies, shoes clipclop on cement again, cars roar past unconcerned, horns, lights, eyes ablaze. Everyone runs for the last train home, hoping it hasn't left.

Some adhere to each other in pairs, playing at hands, rubbing hips and lips, sweaty fingers ply in and out of each other while shoulders play on a pendulum. On their faces a satisfied, semi-contented smile spreads, a masque of success, as they, in ark fashion, plod off light of heart and head, two by two, wondering. But others are alone. Their faces tell stories of search, their eyes tales of solitude on a Saturday night. Hands thrust deep into sweaty pockets, men stare and comment, sing and howl, back pat and love pat as they stand watching the passing mobs. Single women flash a naked knee and a carefully exposed or outlined bust or butt, then ignore comments and turn suddenly aloof when an admirer expresses his approval. Some stand in front of banks in the dark and talk in strange voices, others in front of stands where tea and sandwiches roll out like waves into the crowd. Others queue up for food inside, or at machines, thirst and appetites taking first place in a rare contest. Men put their money down, money which is time, time which is life, life which is theirs to bargain with, to "gather and squander," to get gain with, or to lose. That pound for which he worked four hours he spends in a moment of generosity on his drinking friends. Four hours he worked for a pint and some conversation, bad air, and passing disputes over God or home. A half day on the expense account, a meal on the grocery bill, a night's sleep on the body—all for that hour or two of contact over a community cup of ale. Outside, the shop windows gleam on into the night, lights change at the corner, crosswalk tides rise and fall, and in the middle of the mass, I saw a crippled woman in a brown full-length coat crossing the road. Her four feet of stature measured by her three feet of oak walking stick was small, and her hunched back made her appear even closer to the ground.

Bob Caulfield, soft-spoken Christian anthropologist who majored in clinical psychology at Oklahoma found himself alone, without his family in an apartment house just off Edgware Road in London. After college he maneuvered his way to Afghanistan, where he discovered a need for English-Persian texts. So, he returned to Michigan, did a masters degree in Linguistics, went back to Afghanistan and wrote English-Persian texts which are now used in Afghanistan schools. Especially interested in syntax and morphology, he then, after spending seven years in that country and having three children, decided to return to Michigan to do a doctorate in Anthropology. They were all very happy in Ann Arbor. The doctorate thesis is still undecided, but he is considering in a sort of unqualified way a study of the political forces in three Afghan (as he now calls them) villages in a valley. Misgivings about his ability and readiness to do doctorate work plagued him when we met, not because he had no past success, but because of the sudden and eye-opening contact with such a huge body of knowledge that includes the political and social history of the Middle East, Islam, French, and related topics. But, when tired of all that and the lecture notes and room, he either sought out the Estonian who could hardly speak English, the 50-year-old New Zealand doctor, or the story-telling Mrs. Chambers, a modern Moll Flanders full of tales and woe, wit and show, a life that could prove to be great material.

6-6-66 Earl's Court

The Olivetti is back. Enrolled in short story class at City Literary Institute. Wrote a 4,000 word short story about James Tyler, a university student home on vacation who accidentally discovers his actual paternity while rummaging around in the family attic with his girlfriend one rainy afternoon. Adults in the class mocked me for hyperbole and overstating the significance of falsified birth records. "Being a bastard or adopted just makes you more interesting," one woman said. Learned a lot but didn't like the oral critique of the first draft of "Put Away Childish Things." (They were right, but I didn't go back for more insults.) Other than for mechanical problems, I prefer written notes on paper or margin rather than jokes and public proclamation about all my shortcomings as a writer. As a novice, art is a private undertaking. Just kept writing and revising and wandering the city while Cheney was at work.

Submitted to City Literary Institute ... PUT AWAY CHILDISH THINGS *London, Spring, 1966*
Earl's Court

It was one of those Saturdays in November when rain taps nervous-fingered messages into attics while wind plays silver piccollos through cracks in the siding; A day when children stay inside to play quiet games of adventure and theater, acting out the discoverer and old maid in front of companions or an understanding mirror. Their props are a packrats attic hoard: cedar chests, rusting steel bed steads, yellowing magazines, hat boxes, old stoic portraits. In corners where a certain magneto has drawn stovepipes and old lamps, dust and darkness shakehands in silent laughter. Cavern, monestary, hermitage, museum in which only the outdated, worn, tired, and fading fall silently asleep. When the sun invades through cracks in the shingles, mould-like dust covering surfaces of brown and marroon shines like some light, white, fur. Rafters run their inverted V to union, and from those roof ribs drying bulbs and dying dresses hang. Order here is foreign, chaos a mute demagogue. History of the house slumbers here, fragmented, awaiting some prowling curiousity to uncover these retired wittnesses of caprice and grandeur, now asleep on mattresses where condensed water falls. Mud wasps have plastered their nests in obscure niches, rags fill others to keep out the wind. On and old taboret, a square metal picture box with piano hinges sits insignificantly. Dust of the light, white fur blurrs the two people dancing across the Gainsborough scene on the cover, and inside a mirror reflects what it can.

It was on a Saturday afternoon that James Tyler returned to his home beneath that attic, to his parents, to his past. Vacation from the university had allowed a temporary escape, so, after consulting his financee, they decided to spend a few days in the country, then, Susan and his mother could pass solemn judgements without bissection. Everything was easy at the beginning because both James and Susan were perfect visitors: avoiding contraversy, laughing appropriately, avoiding criticism, and prasing properly. Dinner passed with superficialities as a special guest and long interludes of ruffled behind silences as his companion. Finally, with both appetite & propriety satisfied, James spoke:

"Susan and I were thinking it might be exciting to explore the attic. Since it's raining outside, I might be able to find a few of your souvenirs, Dad, and maybe even something new. My father was famous for his wandering travel ways, Sue."

"That was before I met your mother. Was different then."

6-8-66 to 6-14-66 Cycling London to Stonehenge

Left on Wednesday morning the 8th of June—packs, tent, rented bikes, kitten, early streets quiet except for a milkman who whirred along beside us, stopping, smiling, delivering. We thought about stealing cream and yogurt from his electric van, but that seemed like a dishonest beginning to an honest escape. And besides it would have been too heavy and too bulky to carry. Passing through streets lined with buildings, shops unopened, empty sidewalks, and streetlights blinking off and on unseen messages of stop and go. Getting out of the octopus is difficult. Houses repeat themselves along unending blacktop ribbons. Windows stare, gables angle up and down like huge sawteeth against the horizon. We'd planned to start early, but started late without much breakfast. Escape was in our minds and wheels rolled, sprockets flashed, and chains ran steadily for us, unerringly.

At Highway 4: Heading southwest, we stopped for tea and information, two essential ingredients of English wandering. Entering the shop, we forgot to duck, and the kitten drew attention. Tea from a man with clean trousers, a light face and blond beard and mustache that covered his chin and lips like well-combed wool. Without watching the strainer or the tea, he poured the cups full-to-the-brim, smiled, gave a toast order to the kitchen lady, and set up more cups.

At Staines gas station: I asked an attendant resting in his little shack for the fastest way to the country where we could smell some grass, hear a bird sing, and smell a little fresh cows and dew. He bit off some of a pipe stem, spit it out quietly, and as I watched, he pointed without looking at the map and explained where to go. Blue eyes half sunk in a pimpled and pock-marked face, his knees curled up under him, his nose led the way into most of his life and the hairs protruding in grey and white looked like cat's whiskers.

"Now if you go down here to Chertay, and turn off there and head off through here, you should pick up some decent countryside. Where you off to?"

"Heading for Cornwall but don't expect to arrive," I said.

"You head off down through there by Ottershaw, and you'll find just what you lookin' for. Stay off a those main roads, those red ones there, 'cause traffic on them is thicker than fleas."

"Is that the main road south?"

"Right. You want to stay away from it. Main roads are always bad, everybody in a hurry."

"Ok, mate," I said, and we rode out.

Crossed the River Staine: Saw white swans and good rowboats. Riding in a basket lashed to the back of Cheney's bike, the kitten kept climbing out onto Cheney's back and crawling up under her hair. That little beast wasn't much fun. Rolled down past the odor of pigs and cows in green fields. We were getting away from the octopus.

At Chertsey: We stopped in a playground where a woman pushed her children in a swing. There, the kitten got out, scampered about exploring, while we rested and looked at the rhododendrons in bloom, the green oval garden in front.

Through Ottershaw: Burrowhill, Chobham, West End, Donkey Town, Camberley, all flash by now, their suburban gardens almost quiet, deserted places. A firing range on one side with skeletons of burned-out tanks where once men played at war; signs posted tell of the unexploded dangers of mortars and grenades still lurking there and that one must not touch anything or proceed beyond a certain point marked by flags.

On top of a hill: We made camp. Some people stopped and backed their car into the trees, hid the trunk, and started eating a picnic lunch, an escapist weekend that they had planned for months, but they were inside the firing range.

At the bottom of a nameless hill: We stopped to ask a woman for water: she offered a cup of tea to send us on our way, but I refused politely, walked out and forgot my cork for the canteen. While I stood outside drinking, a little boy came out and bashfully handed me the cork stopper which threw me clear back to Porto where the shoulders of highways covered with cork helped me walk and make a song.

At a farm: I watched a farmer repair and replace the straw thatch and woven wire on his roof. "It's the bloody birds move in," he told me. Not much had changed—as the old saying goes, "A mile from London is a year back in time." More true in some areas than others.

In a quiet pub: I tried a pint and what they called a Scotch egg and Cheney had a shandy. Always there were more directions, permission to camp in barns, invitations to breakfast or dinner or tea. No shortage of generosity.

Along English backroads: The riding was easy going most days; there were always ancient ups and downs, but most roads are smooth blacktop, some shaded, and hedgerows run wild lines over all the green sculptured vegetation.

On a remote green ridge: One afternoon, I biked ahead of Cheney, came to a fork in the road. With Cheney out of sight behind me, I decided to explore the fork leading right off the main route. After what I thought was a short side trip, I returned to the main route, but Cheney was no where in sight. I waited at that junction for her to appear, but fearing a mishap I backtracked on the main road. Didn't find her anywhere within reason, so returned to the junction and assuming she was now ahead of me, I pedaled double time until I caught up with her resting and indignant and modestly furious beside the road.

"How'd you get behind me? Where'd you go?" she demanded.

"I took that side road, then came back."

"I thought you were ahead of me and I couldn't catch up."

"I'm sorry. I waited for you, but I didn't see you go by that junction."

"Well, we better stick together from now on."

"Yeah, I'm sorry. I was just curious," I said.

At Upton Grey: We met a retired Englishman and his wife. Their house was named, "The Case is Altered." Their two dogs pursued a hedgehog while we enjoyed an evening of conversation and brandy. Something unforgettable about that quiet hospitable time at Upton Grey where four roads met and crossed in a hollow on a sunny English afternoon.

Around Windsor: One morning on our return trip, Cheney and I were camped in the tent in a kind farmer's barn. Peaceful place, skin to skin, side by side, warm and cozy in the sleeping bag—even the kitten slept in that morning. After I woke up, Cheney's head and black hair were close to me when I saw something strange and surreal and unbelievable right in front of me—Cheney's hair was crawling with tiny red insects. Agggh! I looked at my forearm cradling Cheney's head. My skin was crawling with unknown red insects. Should I wake her now or let her sleep, then wake and make love before breakfast? Thousands of spider mites took over that morning. Cheney was apologetic. Apparently, the kitten she bought from the RSPCA had given the spider mites to us—every body part everywhere. We turned our tired spokes toward London. After returning the rented bikes, the first stop was the chemist where Cheney knew what we needed—a liquid called Detol. A shower or two of red Detol became our finale. We had to feed a lot of sixpence to the on-demand shower. All in all, we reached Stonehenge and returned, covered approximately 215 miles in six days, our speed slowed by our being a bit overweight, sore, out of shape, and covered with mites.

6-26-66 Reykjavik, Iceland (airport), Postcard Home

London is four hours behind, New York 4 hours ahead. Will buy bus ticket in NYC and head west looking for work. Liz has stayed [in London] to study. Will write along the way. Iceland is volcanic, patches of snow, patriotic, Norse, brooding, Beowulfian. [Bananas grow at the edge of the arctic circle.]

GAV

6-27-66 to 6-30-66 New York to Fargo, ND

Landed in NY. Home again but glad to get out of NYC. Had enough money for a bus ticket to Fargo, North Dakota. Nothing to eat for three days. In Fargo, went to police station, asked permission to sleep overnight in the jail. Granted.

This morning went to farmer's café, got a job bucking bales for Red River Valley ranch. Hot and heavy three-wire bales in 95 to 110 heat. I'm out of shape. Good big farm lunch. Earned $15 which was nearly the death of me, not to speak of my back. A swim and shower afterwards eased everything. Made enough to buy a bus ticket to Spokane. Cool Grayhound. Sleepy. Wondering about Lisa [*nickname for Cheney a.k.a. Liz, Lisa, Elizabeth*]. Writing in my journal again.

7-2-66 Letter from Cheney in London to George in Spokane

[Opened by parents before 7/20, the day received by George.]

Dear George

Forgive me for not wishing you a cosy flight & a hot cup of tea on your arrival in Iceland but my heart was too heavy & my tongue tied in knots & I do hope you realised that I wished you a very very bon flight, from the tips of my toes (which is much lower than the bottom of my heart although perhaps not as poetic).

The tube trip back to the flat was a blank, night fell I think as everything was a black mass, however as black masses seem to open up so did this one & the view of my bright room was blurred by tears, & so between these tears I unpacked & stashed away all my goodies & as I look at the room today I congratulate myself for I find that the job has been done rather well.

You foresaw a loneliness for me & I felt much more; sadness, loneliness? a longing much greater than the mind can withstand & I yearned for the end to the sensations that my mind & body were being subjected to.

The Diary of Anne Frank seems to me to be an odd choice of book from your library to use as a diversion from my thoughts. I wonder why I chose it & the reason may be because it is familiar to me & retains a memory of cheerfulness, anyway the diversion worked although at 9:15 pm I was watching the clock with the knowledge of your arrival in Iceland & I wondered about that nice hot cup of tea & the baggage problem you would be facing before your next departure at 12:15 am. My head popped out of the book again at 12:15 & I saw you safely on the plane bound for that familiar New York. How you spent those extra three hours in Iceland between both flights I can only surmise & my guess is that you spent it with a traveling companion.

It was 7 am before I awakened this morning [July 2] & I certainly felt much brighter as I think you were safely out of New York in that cosy bus, on your way to a much healthier environment. As you can guess I ate that big juicy grapefruit for breakfast before going to the bank this morning & I thank god that this trip was made necessary as I "crashed" into Clare and Bugalugs who had both come into my tramping grounds for the same reason as I, & so ended my depression. Clare had just returned from the

Continent, as had Bugalugs so I came face to face with two brown and friendly faces—coincidence? Mentioning co-incidence I wonder about my meeting with Mrs. Coss as I submerged from Earl's Court Station accompanied by Clare & bound for Clare's flat on a social visit. how with your imagination you can just see it.

Mrs. Coss—You left rather hastily yesterday
Feeble me—Yes we were in a hurry.
Mrs. Coss—You know of course that the 70.00 must be paid.
Me—Yes
Mrs. Coss—Where are you living?
Me After—In the Cumberland Hotel for tonight only.
Mrs. Coss—& after that?
Clare—With me!
Mrs. Coss—And where might that be?
Me—20 Courtfield Gardens
Mrs. Coss—I shall call upon you tonight. Of course you realize that the trunk and rubbish will have to be disposed of by you!
Me—My husband will be returning for it on Tuesday, which is our official departing date
Mrs. Coss—Stumped
Me—Quick exit at full steam ahead

One more chapter in what I am not sure is a closed book: A thriller I think, I hope it doesn't turn out to be a police file novel—shouldn't enjoy that as much.

A very pleasant day spent with Clare & Bugalugs & I feel that I talked my head off & as I sit here to-night pouring my feelings into this letter to you I feel benefitted beyond words. Not only was it a successful day mentally but I profited financially as well for I have registered once again with a very good nursing agency & have received a cute little uniform of nylon fabric & consists of a blue underdress with a cute little detachable apron & white nylon cap. Now for the good juicy bit—five nights work commencing on Wednesday at King's College Hospital Intensive Care Therapy Unit for coronary occlusion patients & opportunity to observe the modern techniques of heart surgery—well I'm tickled pink with yellow spots.

Why have I decided to continue nursing? The reason is because I feel I must give someone something special & you are too far away I shall give once more a part of me that experience has shown to be well received & which I can give with both love and care. There is also an opportunity for me to work for 'Problems Limited" at 6/ an hour, part time doing the oddest jobs, walking dogs, exercising horses, minding children, oh lots of them.

It is late now so I shall get some sleep in this huge bed of mine, do you think I have a right to ask for two extra blankets?

As I have no postal address to you I may send the letters to your Mum to forward onto you where you are working.

Love,

Lisa XXXX

7-2-66 Letter from George in Fargo to Cheney in London

[*Unreceived.*]

Dear Lisa—

You are here; your vision and feeling has become mine; your love, your laugh are ever present, almost ghost-like haunting my mind at dusk and dawn. Time past has influenced time future and time present as T.S. Eliot said it does. Horses, murky cups of tea, tennis, medicine, Australia, kittens: all have more meaning, almost reminders of the times of 6 Courtfield Gardens. Even my suit brought your dimples and lace running, panting back; evenings, candlelight cherry, crab, conversation and colors of your hair in sunlight. I cannot escape your mystery, our history, because I see now the meaning of our long tennis game.

I cannot condemn you for not knowing because your humanity and beauty are too great. You, my beauty from Athens, house more than temples ever held. Please, Lisa, remain unmoved from the pillars of innocence.. Experience supports more but loves less. When I arrived here on Saturday, my wish was you transplanted here. Now, I would hesitate to bring you here or ask you to come. We must go away, together, alone, when love is ready to harvest.

If I pour myself out to you, I trust you will know the reason for my spilling over onto you: that is me. You think of me as I think of myself. My parents are still playing the song of life on one string, one Puritan string, that plays no soothing music to my soul. Only discord is their song, what is wrong with man, his sin not beauty, condemnation of the emotional, ignorance of the scientific. On and on into drumming goes their mind.

And now you, my love, what about you? Is the world kind to you there now? Is your life full? Do you smile and laugh and talk as before? Have you found people, friends? Do you fill your days with thoughts and actions you love? Oh Lisa, Lisa, my hope is mountainous for your good mind, health and spirit! Faith in you is strong and yet I know you were affected by my withdrawal. It hurt when you ran from me at the air port. I knew you could not stay, but some force made me hold until my time had ended.

Love, George

7-3-66 Fargo to Spokane

[*Unreceived letter from George to Cheney.*]

Dear Lisa—

Today, Sunday, was the day to please parents, as I have told you, and that is what it was. Dressing up, being proper, son-like, obedient. First thing my father did was chop off all my hair, making me after the typical image, his image again. So, I laugh quietly to myself, act my role, and long for your ear to whisper in about what is happening.

Montana's plains were your dreamland: horses everywhere, blue sky that's too big to eat with my hungry eyes. Never have I been happier than when the quiet, calm, peaceful solitude of prairie and mountains met. Sweet clover, delicate yellow flowers beside the road paint there with the heavy scent of honey. Sage's strong odor breaks through it all while meadow larks sing alone on fence posts. Write, Lisa, Please!

Love, George

7-5-66 Letter from Cheney in London

[Opened by parents before 7/20, the day received by George.]

Dear George—

There is a confession I am making to you & I hope you will understand. When you left I felt that you had more than a suspicion of the fact that I am pregnant & I felt that I could not confess this fact to you as you would have to decide your feelings toward the problem immediately & hence halt your return to the life that you want. You did not ask me directly & I felt that you did not want to know the truth. It is strange but I felt so near to you & thought I knew your problems & difficulties you had.

Upon further consideration I realized that my imagination had perhaps run off & therefore I had no right to fill in the open spaces of the conversation that I had with myself & that perhaps you really did not know.

There was also the terrible memory I had of the statement made by you about the girls who deliberately do this sort of thing to men & I did not want to be thought of in that way by you, as this bewilders me as much as you. Therefore on those grounds I decided to have the babe in England & not tell you about it until after you had completed your final exams, which will co-incide with the new arrival. Hence enabling you to be free of worry & so that you could get a good pass. That was my decision.

According to the doctor I have not the right to make such a decision for you or the baby nor to assume anything of anyone:

(1) It would mean robbing you of a great experience
(2) The power of decision is the characterization of each individual.
(3) The child would be illegitimate & fatherless & I guess you know only too well the feeling of incompleteness in this type of life.
(4) There is no substitute for a real mother or real father in any child's eyes

Well so much for my decision for I find that I am not the judge? So I tell you the truth knowing that you will give it a lot of thought & please do not regret your decision because your life is too important to me to be barred by a shot-gun wedding though only God knows how I love you. There are of course two other alternatives

(1) Adoption by a British family—rejected by me.
(2) Abortion was offered by means of tablets or by an intra-venous injection @25.00—rejected by me.

What is your decision on these alternatives? I feel that I know already that it will be as mine. So the fact remains that I shall have the child & love him as I love you. Again nationality is another problem (3) & the Dr has advised me to get off British soil and immigrate to Canada to the unmarried mothers association, otherwise there will be difficulties later, I don't understand exactly.

Well, I am undecided, perhaps I should confide in John as I can't go back to Australia, I guess it is because I will not admit my mistakes & get the family ridiculed. If it had been purposeful, I could go back with my head held high & they couldn't touch me. No I don't want to tell my brothers either as I feel you understand more than anyone of my family & if I tell them it may cause too much trouble. No shall just tell you as I am so alone now, can't tell the girls because their tongues are too loose.

All my pourings upon you must feel like a thunderstorm to you & although I am terribly frightened of what lies ahead I am also happy that I have something of you. Also no money problems as I can get my teeth fixed for nix & free medical expenses & a good salary for a couple of months. Oh & of course there is the savings on chocolate as I'm restricted to a pure food diet, doesn't worry me strangely enough.

Oh there are so many things I have to say to you—yes, the landlord fixed the window & some nice breezes come in both evening & early morning. Also I have the jazziest light so beautifully bright that it could light up the whole of London. Thank you for giving my room your little piece of tiger touch as it is a great comfort to me, even though he does look unfriendly.

Unfortunately schooling is out of the question now & I feel so sad about that as I feel I would do a fine job & meet so many nice people. Oh well exams would be done in the maternity ward & that would be funny to see.

Clare and I were lined up at the tube on Monday at Piccadilly Circus. She put her hand into her pocket & pulled out a one shilling piece & a peseta [Spanish coin] & as we noticed that the sizes of each coin were identical we decided to put the peseta in & see if we received a ticket. 6 pm peak hour you can imagine it—the machine started spitting out tickets all over the floor & wouldn't stop, oh such a sight & it made a frightful noise. Clare grabbed two tickets & fled, the crowd was gathering so I grabbed a ticket & fled also, boy did I go fits of laughter thought I would pop my seams.

Well today being Tuesday [5th], I was on my way to the nursing agency & my registration number in hand to give to the principal I "crashed" into Therese who informed me that Marjorie would be at Clare's apartment all day hoping that I may make the journey across to Earl's Court. Co-incidence, I don't know because I had no previous intentions of going today. However it was great to see her & hear her recent experiences in Greece & on the "Ellinis" from England to Australia as a ship's nurse. She is flying to Ontario next week to join "Digby" whom I have mentioned to you & they shall get married. Only six weeks inclusive to emigrate so she leaves next week & has left their address.

I am parting from your company at this moment until later as this is the biggest letter that I have ever written—sure hope it doesn't ground the aeroplane.

May our special God be with you.

Love,

"Lisa" XXXXXXX

7-9-66 Letter to Cheney from George at Bruce Mackey Ranch

[*Unreceived.*]

Dear Lisa—

I'm working at the Bruce Mackey ranch (brand NP) just 38 miles south of Spokane among the fertile but rocky hills of southwestern Washington. Here, men rise with the sun and chickens, work with machines and hands, and sleep the sleep of youth exhausted. Days are spent now in the harvest of baled hay, which means cutting, raking, baling, hauling, stacking for $12.00 per day plus room and board. Outside there are three horses corralled, a mare and two stallions, up the road about 200 chickens squawk, back this way 20 pigs walk in their food, two dogs defend the white ranch house and a spooky black cat hunts the barn. I came here 3 days ago to work about two weeks before going on south to do wheat harvest work for $20 per day plus room and board.

Smells of sweet clover fill the night, crickets and coyotes sing weird duets, and I wonder how the deer and two fawns will pass the night out there on the range. Days are hot, about 80-85 degrees, nights are cool, I am well, slim as I was in Spain, and driving truck, throwing bales around, learning about these men, their loves and sorrows. One is a retired cowboy, the other a bachelor of 74; both slow-talking, hard-riding men who speak of the good old days more than once during dinner. I pretend to be illiterate harvest hobo.

Love, Lisa, I long to see the sunlight's gentle rays fall on your body, on your raven hair, on your eyes of cat and kindness. Hope tells me you are well, but if I think I cry and curse fate because of the distance that now separates us. To know that you smile, are happily occupied, love me, and your worlds of people and animals, blue sky, and the delicate flower of yellow and gold, would all be as finding bird song in an early morning near Basingstoke. But then fear springs up because I know nothing of your mind and yet I longingly wish myself and yourself together again as before. Please, Lisa, speak to me or I shall return to ask of your lips, words and kisses as before.

Love, George

7-12-66 Letter from Cheney in London to George

[Opened by parents before 7/20, the day received by George.]

Dearest George—

I hope this finds you happy and well. I'm still working in London and miss you to bits. I wanted you to know I finished the Anne Frank diary that you gave me that day we moved my stuff to that new flat. I didn't stay there very long because I'm pregnant. Actually, I was pregnant before you left, and you kind of surprised me when you said nothing about it. Sorry I didn't tell you. I guess you couldn't tell. So I went to see a social worker and we talked over the situation. She advised me not to have the baby in England for lots of reasons including citizenship. She also said I should include you in any decision. As the father, you have as much right as I do.

You said you would find a job someplace, so I can't contact you now. I sent an earlier letter to your home address—the one you gave me in Spokane. Instead of waiting for your answer, I decided I should come to the States so we can talk this over. I bought passage on a cruise ship, and by the time you read this, I might be somewhere on the Atlantic between London and Montreal. From landing, I'll go across Canada on the bus to the US. That might take 3 days. Not sure exactly when I'll arrive but my two letters will be waiting for you. I'll call your folks to let them know I'm coming.

All my love, Liz

7-20-66 Mackay Ranch to South Crescent, Spokane

Came home from ranch. Tired from 10 days stacking bales in July heat. Just got in the door, put down my suitcase when Mom hands me three opened letters from Lisa and says, "You better read these. Sorry I opened them. They looked important." There's no welcome home. It's like an order, a command. Her voice is low and intense. So I go into the back yard and read them all. Shocked, surprised, dumbfounded—what can I say or do? I'm almost in tears. My throat swells, chokes. After Lisa ran from me and left me standing alone at the London airport without saying goodby, I never expected to see her again. We had a short intense affair in Spain and I knew she wasn't pregnant when we separated after traveling together and she returned to England.

Sitting there in shock, I remembered that day in Alicante when she asked a Dutch guy named Lex Van to ask me what my intentions were. I'd told him we were getting to know each other. I was serious about her. I wrote my parents they might have a new daughter-in-law. She was my first profound sexual experience; I was not hers. Worried about pregnancy during those first two weeks together on the beach, I always withdrew before ejaculation. "No time for babies," I told her. She always tried to stop me.

Hand shaking, I stare at the words: "I thought you knew I was pregnant." My eyes blur and tear. I didn't know anything. She knew and didn't tell until she wrote and sent these letters. And there was no way to contact each other: I was out working at the ranch and she had left London. Now, she's coming south from Canada by bus tomorrow. She's pregnant. Mom listened while I returned a call from Montreal to her, invited her to stay here. Indignation is in the air.

7-29-66 Wedding Day: 3615 South Crescent Avenue, Spokane

Whole story can never be told. While the reel recorder turned round and round, it created the tape of the wedding for Lisa's mother in Australia. Spoke into the microphone to the absent Australian audience. Standing together in my parents' front room—Lisa and I holding onto the same knife handle—we announced our cutting the first slices of that huge round white-frosted wedding cake. Vows but no rings exchanged. Dad took the pictures. It was all we knew of love at that moment. Lisa has a profession. She's a beautiful woman. Everyone can see that. Says she has a special God, says she loves me to bits. I'm broke. I'm going to be a senior English major in college. I have no tuition. I have no profession, no visible means of support. I ate our wedding cake and ice cream and drank sweet punch, and ironically wondered if I would ever be ready for this middle class marriage or parenthood or both. There in my parents' living room, it was all daunting. In one letter, Lisa called it all "bewildering." I wanted to go away, but knew I couldn't leave until the service was over and recorder turned off. I watched Lisa study the carefully arranged teaspoons and folded napkins on the white linen table cloth. She has "get rich" fantasies about life in America. She could lie with a straight face to a British landlord. I love Lisa and accept the consequence of our love on the beach. She's made all the decisions now. We're together. We would be parents in a year. I would be a father at 22—a huge and sudden change. We would just try to learn and understand and tolerate the differences between us obscured by education and passion and life on the road. For wedding gifts, my parents gave us new tennis rackets—gut strings, a can of three balls. They drove us to a strange motel west of town. Different passion—sex strange now. Everything changed. Letters are bombs. She can't forget how I once denounced women who use sex to force marriage. What can I say? Spain far away now. She's here. Feel alien. Don't think I'll write any more.

VERTICAL FROM UPPER LEFT:
Bride and Groom with candelabra
(photo credit: Rev. Frank Venn)
newly weds on the couch
(photo credit: Joe Sander)

VERTICAL FROM UPPER RIGHT:
Bride and Groom cutting the cake
(photo credit: Rev. Frank Venn)
newly weds on the couch
(photo credit: Joe Sander)

Books by George Venn

POETRY

Lichen Songs: New and Selected Poems

West of Paradise: New Poems

Marking the Magic Circle: An Intimate Geography (multi-genre) (with photographer Jan Boles)

Off the Main Road (with artist Don Gray)

Sunday Afternoon: Grande Ronde (with artist Ian Gatley)

NON FICTION

Beaver's Fire: A Regional Portfolio (1970-2010)

Keeping the Swarm: New and Selected Essays

Darkroom Soldier: Photographs and Letters from the South Pacific Theater World War II. With Frederick H. Hill

Soldier to Advocate: C. E. S. Wood's 1877 Legacy

WORKS EDITED

Brock Evans: *Endless Pressure, Endlessly Applied: The Autobiography of an Eco-Warrior*

Stephani Stephenson, *Hearthfire*

Daniel S. Pokorney, *Tragedy to Grace*

Fred Hill: *A Photographer's Life*

The *Oregon Literature Series*, Vols. 1–6

WORKS EDITED *(cont.)*

Amelia Diaz Ettinger, *Speaking at a Time* (poems and Spanish translations)

Lars Nordstrom, *Ten New Lives: Swedes in the Pacific Northwest*

Lars Nordstrom, *The Procession of Memories: Selected Poems 1929–1945.* By Harry Martinson. Edited and Translated by Lars Nordstrom.

Pulling Together: An Anthology of Baker County Poetry. Baker City, OR: Baker County Library, 1998.

River Hills Rounded With Wind. With Paulann Petersen. The Dalles, OR: Dalles, Wasco County Library, 1998.

"Introduction: The Woodcutter Liu Hai Plays with the Golden Toad." Yi Wen-zhang. *Folklore India* 27.1 (Jan. 1986): 3–13, 17.

"Carolyn Kizer: An Interview with Tim Barnes." *Oregon East* 15. (1984): 41–50.

"Richard Hugo-Ron Bayes Interview." *Oregon East* 13. (1982): 41–52.

Eastern Oregon Literary Supplement, 1972, 1973, 1974. La Grande: Western Communications/Oregon Arts Commission.

Co-Editor for *Prospectus* Magazine, Caldwell, The College of Idaho, 1965.

Sports Editor, *Tesemini* 1961. Spirit Lake, ID: Spirit Lake High School, 1961.

About the Author (1943–)

George Andrew Fyfe was conceived in the Nisqually River watershed—south of Mt. Rainier National Park. After his father died suddenly in 1944, he was raised until school age by his maternal grandparents among the evergreen Cascades, in their family apiary, on their rural homestead, and by a strong work ethic—all augmented by musical and King James traditions. In 1947, his mother married Rev. Frank Venn, a strict conservative Presbyterian minister who adopted George and his brother, thus changing their names to Venn. In 1957 his new family moved from the coast to the gold larch mountains of Spirit Lake, Idaho where, as student body president, George graduated in 1961, then accepted an athletic scholarship to The College of Idaho. Foregoing athletics, he worked summers as a beekeeper, logger, lineman, office manager, and during undergraduate years as stage manager, tennis player, actor, baritone soloist, choir manager, and finally a literary editor.

As a freshman he published his first fiction in *Prospectus*, the campus literary magazine. Still undecided about a major after his sophomore year, he flew to Ecuador to manage an office, perfect his Spanish, teach ESL for USIS, coach a basketball team, and sing on radio and television. Those months living free from family and cultural constraints, he began to write long letters on his Olivetti portable, a process he found gave him direction, inspiration, and discovery. Returning to The College of Idaho, he declared an English major, published another short story, then inspired by his Ecuadorian awakening, he decided to study in Spain. That year abroad is the subject of this 2023 book.

In 1967, he enrolled in the University of Montana MFA program, where he continued to write short fiction while also maintaining his diverse intellectual interests in culture, history, languages, music, conservation, and regional literatures. In his first graduate course he studied with Harold G. Merriam, renowned northwest literary editor. In courses with Richard Hugo and Madeline De Frees, he wrote his first poems. *Garret*, the university magazine, solicited and published his first literary fiction, and *Montana the Magazine of Western History* published his first northwest history. Continuing to write both non-fiction prose and short fiction with William Kittredge, he completed a historical novella, a dialogue between literature and history, an essay on the Arabic article in English, a linguistic analysis of Conrad's use of Spanish, and many short stories. Employed as a trained beekeeper during graduate school, those skills converged with reading Aldo Leopold and the wilderness conservation movement. In the decades that followed, he would publish testimony, lectures, and articles on conservation, and for five years, he led the successful opposition to the dam on Catherine Creek in Oregon.

Graduating with an MFA in 1970, he moved his Australian wife, son, and daughter to the Grande Ronde Valley in eastern Oregon to accept an academic position at Eastern Oregon College (now Eastern Oregon University), a small, underfunded, remote, 4-year institution east of the Cascades. Over the next two decades, while developing and publishing as a writer, editor, and poet, he taught and administered the Creative Writing program, served as impresario for the *Ars Poetica* literary reading series, and adviser to *Oregon East*, the campus literary magazine. An outspoken untenured part-time professor working under largely privative conditions, he hosted many campus readings by nationally recognized poets and writers. Off campus, his multi-genre collection *Marking the Magic Circle* was honored with an Oregon Book Award; his poetry was praised and published in two books and won a national Pushcart Prize. As a regional literary activist, he published reviews, lectured, adjudicated competitions, collected folklore, advocated for arts and humanities programs, and taught the first courses in Western and Native American literatures.

In 1981–1982, he became one of the first American writers to teach English in post-Cultural Revolution China. Returning from teaching at South China University, he directed the Composition Program, and in 1988, he was asked to design and direct the new ESL (writing) program. That same year, after seventeen years without tenure, he resigned from his Creative Writing responsibilities.

In the early 1990s Venn twice conducted the "Baden-Württemberg/Oregon Exchange Program," a three-week international orientation seminar for German graduate students. Continuing to write and publish, he held offices and served on the boards of literary, historical, environmental, cooperative, and educational organizations. In 1995, he was honored with the *Andres Berger Award in Poetry* by Northwest Writers Inc. For years, he also served on the executive committee and later as President of the Oregon Council of Teachers of English. As General Editor, he also designed and directed the nationally-recognized *Oregon Literature Series* (Vols. 1–6), the definitive historical anthology of Oregon literature. His work has been honored with numerous awards including the Stewart Holbrook Award for "outstanding contributions to Oregon's literary life."

After receiving the 2002 Distinguished Teaching Award from Eastern Oregon University, Venn resigned to actively continue writing, editing, and publishing. In this decade, he has published two historical works, a volume of personal essays, and a 460-page portfolio of northwest literary history. His poems have been included in 17 state, regional, and national anthologies, carved in stone, set to music by composers, included in feature films. In 2005, the Oregon Cultural Heritage Commission again recognized *Marking the Magic Circle* as "one of the 100 best Oregon books in the two centuries." More recently, his monograph *Soldier to Advocate* (2007), his World War II Fred Hill album *Darkroom Soldier* (2008), and *Endless Pressure, Endlessly Applied* (2020) with Brock Evans have all earned high praise. In 2017, he was honored with the Lifetime Achievement Award by The College of Idaho, and by the publication of *Lichen Songs: New and Selected Poems*, his most recent book. "The Literary Lion of La Grande," a short film by Eric Schultz, can be viewed on Venn's website: www.georgevenn.com.

6/19/23

For additional copies of this book or to see a full list of
available titles from Wake-Robin Press, please visit:
www.wakerobinpress.com

www.ingramcontent.com/pod-product-compliance
Lightning Source LLC
Chambersburg PA
CBHW040928240426
43667CB00025B/2983